T0013554

SPOOKY
North Carolina

SPOOKY
North Carolina

Tales of Hauntings, Strange Happenings,
and Other Local Lore

SECOND EDITION

RETOLD BY S. E. SCHLOSSER
ILLUSTRATED BY PAUL G. HOFFMAN

Globe
Pequot
ESSEX, CONNECTICUT

Globe Pequot

An imprint of Globe Pequot, the trade division of
The Rowman & Littlefield Publishing Group, Inc.
4501 Forbes Blvd., Ste. 200
Lanham, MD 20706
www.rowman.com

Distributed by NATIONAL BOOK NETWORK

British Library Cataloguing in Publication Information available

Library of Congress Cataloging-in-Publication Data available

ISBN 978-1-4930-4489-4 (paper) | ISBN 978-1-4930-4490-0 (ebook)

∞™ The paper used in this publication meets the minimum requirements
of American National Standard for Information Sciences—Permanence of
Paper for Printed Library Materials, ANSI/NISO Z39.48-1992.

For my family: David, Dena, Tim, Arlene, Hannah,
Seth, Emma, Nathan, Ben, Deb, Gabe, Clare,
Jack, Chris, Karen, Davey, and Aunt Mil.

And for all the wonderful folks at Globe
Pequot Press, with my thanks.

For Karl and Cres Schultz, with my thanks for
their hospitality. For Robbie, who tells a great story.
And for Paul Roache and Gregory Brown, for their
warm Boone welcome and wonderful tales.

Contents

Contents

Contents

SPOOKY SITES . . .

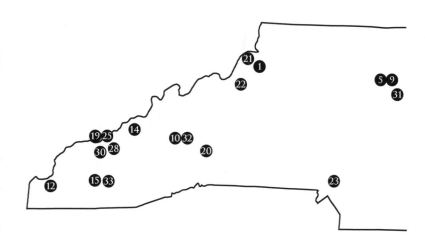

❶	Boone	❿	Asheville
❷	Raleigh	⓫	Wilmington
❸	Ocracoke	⓬	Murphy
❹	Maco	⓭	Madison
❺	Winston-Salem	⓮	Cataloochee
❻	Greensboro	⓯	Nantahala National Forest
❼	Dare County	⓰	Chapel Hill
❽	Goldsboro	⓱	Elizabeth City
❾	Winston-Salem	⓲	Fayetteville

AND WHERE TO FIND THEM

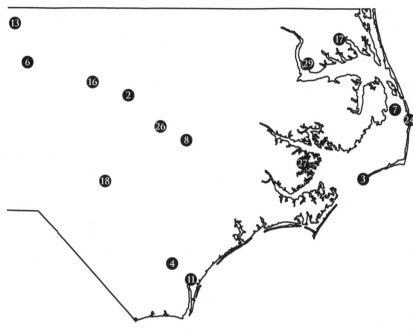

⑲ Great Smoky Mountains
National Park

⑳ Bat Cave

㉑ Watauga County

㉒ Pineola

㉓ Charlotte

㉔ Outer Banks

㉕ Great Smoky Mountains
National Park

㉖ Smithfield

㉗ Vandemere

㉘ Cherokee

㉙ Edenton

㉚ Swain County

㉛ High Point

㉜ Asheville

㉝ Franklin

Introduction

The cool sea breeze tangled softly in my hair and brushed across my face as I stepped out of the car. I barely noticed, my eyes fixed in awe on the massive black-and-white-striped Bodie Island Lighthouse looming over the clearing among its outbuildings, framed by the blue sky. The wind was whistling through the tall grass that lined the sand dunes behind the lighthouse and rustling in the trees as I pulled all my photography equipment out of the car and started snapping pictures in the warm January sunlight.

Bodie Lighthouse—which stands in Hatteras Island National Seashore in North Carolina—hadn't even been on my list of Things to Do when I set out from my gorgeous Outer Banks vacation "home away from home" that morning. My mind was all caught up in the excitement of visiting the Wright Brothers monument and seeing the First Flight exhibit at Kitty Hawk. I spent the whole morning re-creating the First Flight in my mind, walking the exact spot where the very first plane had taken off and landed under its own power, and watching in approval as a small-prop plane landed on the small airstrip next door. It seemed fitting to me that this place should still be used as an airstrip.

All at once, I felt tired and hungry. I had done enough research for one morning. Leaving the Wright Brothers behind, I sat down to a nice leisurely lunch and then realized that the rest of the day was unplanned! This was a happy occurrence during my normally rushed spooky research trip. Getting back in my car, I pulled out onto the highway and proceeded to meander through the Outer Banks, stopping wherever my fancy took me. In this serendipitous way, I found a small beach overlooking the massive bridge between two of the Outer Banks islands. A single set of footprints wandered beside the blue waters of the Pamlico Sound, and a single seagull sat on a piling, resting easily in the sunlight. The footprints reminded me of the old folktale still told in this area of a young naval officer who encountered Blackbeard's headless ghost on an empty beach beside the Sound one dark night ("The Nightmare").

Then I found the lighthouse and had an impromptu photo shoot before taking a long walk on the beach. It was cold on the beach in January. I bundled up against the wind and started looking for empty skate cases and seashells along with a few other hearty souls who had ventured this way. I smiled as I strolled the emptiness of the beach, thinking that the current scene was a far cry from the crowds that lined the beaches of Vandermere during a Jubilee, when oxygen levels drop in the sea, causing crabs and flounder and fish of every description to rush for the shore to find more air. The harvest of all this bountiful seafood involved everyone in town, and it was not a good place to lose a small child, as one family had done in a folktale I had collected from the region. Unless, of course, the ghost of your departed mother was there to guide him back to safety ("Jubilee").

My wanderings in North Carolina started long before my happy day on the beach. I entered the state in the west, staying my first night in Boone, where the spirit of a much-loved dog once returned to bid his master farewell and play one final game of "Fetch." From there, my search for spooky folklore took me over Grandfather Mountain and down to the town of Cherokee, situated on the eastern reservation of that great nation. I spent a day there exploring the Smoky Mountains National Park, though I was not privileged to meet the spirit of Tsali, who still stands guard over his people in their mountain homeland ("The Legend of Tsali"). While sad to miss meeting the guardian spirit of the hills, I was very thankful not to encounter "Raven Mockers," those terrible witches who stalk the dying to steal their hearts and with them the remaining days of their lives.

From the far west, I made my way to Asheville, once the home to phony ghost busters who had the tables turned on *them* when they visited a real haunted house ("Busted!"). I then headed to Charlotte to collect tales of long-ago Resurrectionists ("Resurrection"), who learned a hard lesson about the best way to earn spending money. Then it was onward to Winston-Salem to learn more about the ghost of "The Little Red Man," who once haunted the Single Brothers' house. And I found another great Winston-Salem story about the ghost of "Robah," who followed some adventurous college students home one Halloween night and started making mischief in the den.

North Carolina is so full of folktales that I could talk from dusk to dawn without touching on a third of them. There are stories of boo-hags, witches, devils, premonitions, phantom horsemen, doppelgängers, and more. Vengeance is a strong theme in several tales. An older brother kills his sibling and is visited each night by his brother's ghost, who plucks the hair right off his head ("Plucked"). A bride, abandoned at the altar, finally gets her man from beyond the grave ("The Handshake"). And a woman learns the hard way that she shouldn't steal the diamond engagement ring from her dead sister's hand ("I'm So Cold").

I received a warm welcome from everyone I met in North Carolina, and I heard many amazing and, of course, *spooky* stories. I've put my favorites in this collection. Enjoy!

—*S. E. Schlosser*

PART ONE
Ghost Stories

1

Fetch

BOONE

Clyde was the best dog I ever had. He was a black, gray, and tan German shepherd mix with a keen sense of smell and a quirky disposition. I loved him! He was always happy, always friendly. He went to every class I took at Appalachian State University, sitting at my feet and listening intently. After class, we would wander outdoors and play a game of fetch or go for a hike. Sometimes, we even studied. I would have aced every class if the professors had let *Clyde* take the tests.

Well, we graduated—Clyde with top honors, at least among the students—and had a brief hiatus in the Outer Banks. We loved the beaches and the wind and the waves, me and Clyde. But I was a mountain boy at heart, and the yen for the hills grew so strong within me that I came back to Boone. Clyde didn't mind where we were so long as we stuck together. I bought a nice little one-story ranch house with a full basement and, in time, brought home a bride to live there with the two of us. Sadly, my relationship with both Clyde and the little ranch house outlasted my relationship with my wife.

2

I was pretty devastated by the divorce, and it didn't help matters when my best buddy Clyde died of sheer old age. Tough, strong mountain man that I am, I bawled like a baby when I buried old Clyde in the front yard. There had never been another dog quite like him.

I stuck it out in the house for two years after the divorce but finally decided it was time to buy a condo and move on with my life. That little old house had too many memories, and no Clyde to soften them.

My sister and brother-in-law helped me pack up my things. On the day of the move, they loaded up their truck and headed off to the condo, leaving me to finish packing my own truck. I parked it on the street right in front of the house and trotted back and forth with packages and boxes, leaving the big old mirror that was propped opposite the front door for last, since it needed special packaging so that it wouldn't break during the trip.

I was down to the last few items when I stepped out of the door carrying a box and almost tripped over a stick laying smack-dab in the middle of the front walk. I frowned down at it. Where did that come from? It hadn't been there on my last trip out to the truck, and there was no wind that could have knocked it off a tree into the path. It was, I observed casually, just the type of stick that Clyde always favored when we played fetch—about a foot long and an inch thick. The wood had a knot at the center that looked like a cat's eye.

I felt a pang of loss when I saw the stick. Oh, how I missed Clyde. Adjusting the box on my hip, I scooped up the stick and threw it into the backyard, chucking it right over the low roof of the ranch house. Then I walked out to the truck and carefully loaded my box with the others.

Turning, I headed back toward the house to pick up the last few boxes. And there was the stick again, exactly where it had been before. My flesh crawled, and I felt goose bumps rising on my arms and legs. How had it gotten back here? It was the same funny old stick I'd just thrown over the house. I could tell by the knot at its center that looked like a cat's eye. I glanced around the yard, but no one was there. No way to explain the stick.

Hastily, feeling chills all over my skin, I picked it up and threw it over the roof of the house again. Then I headed in the front door. As I did, I glanced in the mirror propped up against the wall. In the bottom corner, standing reflected on the exterior walkway just where the stick had been, stood Clyde. His black and tan ears were pricked, his dark eyes glowed with delight, and his tail was wagging. There was no doubt it was Clyde.

Now I loved that dog more than anything. But seeing his ghost reflected in that mirror seriously freaked me out. I gasped, blinked, and then hurried to the bedroom to grab the final box off the bed. When I returned to the front hallway, there was nothing reflected in the mirror except empty walkway. I snatched up the old mirror any which way, locked the front door with shaking hands, and hurried down the walk to the truck parked out front. I didn't look down. I *really* didn't want to see if the stick was back.

A moment later, I was in the truck with the blasted old mirror tucked against the passenger's seat. My hands were shaking so badly that it took me two tries to get the engine

FETCH

started. Then the truck was in gear, and I was gone. Goodbye, house. Goodbye, old life. I hit my blinker and slowed for the left turn. Just before I rounded the corner, I glanced in the rearview mirror, staring back at the house. Was that a hint of black and tan by the walkway? The swish of a wagging tail?

A car rumbled past, cutting off my view. By the time I could see it again, the yard was empty.

Goodbye, Clyde.

2

Daddy's Visit

RALEIGH

It was a lovely spring afternoon, and I didn't hurry as I closed the front door behind me. I could smell lilacs in the air and stood for a moment on my small front porch breathing in the scent of spring. I heard birds chirping, a crow cawing in the tree, the whiz of a car passing in the street. And another sound, faint but distinct. The regular chuff-chuff sound of an engine warming up next door. I glanced over but saw no car in the driveway. That was odd. Was my new neighbor warming up the car in the garage? No, of course not. Any sensible person knew that was terribly dangerous. Carbon monoxide could build up fast. The car must be pulled up behind the house where I couldn't see it, I decided.

A family of four had moved in next door about six weeks ago—a young couple in their thirties with two adorable little girls. I'd taken over an apple pie and introduced myself, and they seemed friendly enough. The father left for work before sunup each day and came home around three in the afternoon. He usually spent the time before dinner playing with his girls in the backyard while his wife rested or did errands, although for

7

the last couple of days, it was the mother I saw outside in the afternoons.

I meandered down the front steps to my own car, parked out front in anticipation of my busy afternoon. I wanted to run a few errands before I started dinner. I took a last deep breath of lilac-scented air and then jumped into the car and headed off to the grocery store. I ambled my way through my errands, pausing to chat with a friend at the library, compare notes about fruit with a knowledgeable salesperson at the grocery, and discuss the best way to ripen tomatoes with the fellow manning the desk at the post office.

It was after 3:00 p.m. when I pulled into my driveway and parked the car by the back door. As I retrieved my groceries from the trunk, I heard the neighbor's car chuff-chuffing to itself next door. That was odd. Had they just returned from errands, as I had? Surely their car wasn't still warming up after two and a half hours?

Curious, I walked around the house and peered down my neighbor's driveway. I didn't see a car, but I could hear one running in the garage. Chuff-chuff-chuff. Rumble rumble.

I felt my skin prickling all over. It was very dangerous to run a car in an enclosed space. Even more so when the enclosed space was a garage attached to a house. Carbon monoxide could build up really fast. I stood there holding a couple of bags of groceries, wondering what to do. The soft rumbling sound made me uneasy. Abruptly, I dropped the groceries onto my front porch, walked back to their house, and rang the doorbell repeatedly. No answer. I knocked several times, first on the front door and then the back, calling the parents' names. Still no answer.

Now I was really worried. There was no sign of anyone home, and normally the kids would be out playing in the fenced-in backyard at this time of day. I phoned the house. No answer. I phoned both parents' cell phones. I got voice mail.

I couldn't leave things there. A car running in a closed garage was dangerous. Reluctantly, I called the police and explained the situation. They promised to send someone over, and I waited nervously for them on my front porch. It seemed to take forever for the police car with flashing lights to pull up. I ran at once to the car, babbling desperately about how I'd heard the car earlier but hadn't realized it was in the garage until I got home from my errands. "I think it's been running in there for over two hours," I concluded, almost wringing my hands in dread. The officer's face grew grim, but he spoke soothingly to me, asking me to wait for him on the porch. Then he went up to the house. I watched him ring the bell, knock, call. His partner did the same at the back door. Then they forced the garage door open. And found the young father dead in the car. He had committed suicide.

They called at once for an ambulance, and I heard them crashing into the house through the side door. From the sound of their shouts to each other, both little girls were inside the house and were suffering from the effects of carbon monoxide. The officers carried them out to safety, and I hovered in the background, watching helplessly as they did some preliminary first aid. The ambulance arrived within minutes—thank God—and the girls and their father were rushed to the hospital.

The mother arrived home just as the ambulance was pulling away. She ran toward the police officers in hysterics, demanding to know what had happened. She collapsed when she heard the news, and the officers asked me to go with her to the hospital after they had taken a brief statement from her.

On the way to the hospital, she told me she'd spent the day at a local spa. It was a birthday gift from her parents, and her husband had taken the day off to babysit the girls while she was away. Her husband suffered from clinical depression, but he had seemed so much better after they'd moved to the new house. "I never thought he'd do this," she whispered, scrubbing at her cheeks with a tissue.

When we arrived at the hospital, the doctors took the young mother aside and told her that her husband had been declared dead on arrival. As for the girls, the eldest daughter had been playing on the far side of the house from the garage and was the least affected by the carbon monoxide, but the little four-year-old was in a coma and was not expected to come out of it. Even if she did, the damage she appeared to have suffered was so extensive that she would never function normally again.

The young mother fell to pieces when she heard the news, and I felt terribly guilty myself. If only I had investigated the sound of the running car when I first heard it, I might have saved the life of that poor little girl at least. Now her father was dead, and she was dying. I tried to tell myself it was not my fault. But I didn't really believe it.

With my husband's blessing, I spent the night at the hospital with my neighbor and made arrangements for her parents—who lived overseas—to fly into Raleigh as soon as they could get away. When the older daughter was released in the morning, I brought her to our house to stay until her grandparents arrived from Europe. Her mother remained at the hospital night and day, sleeping in the pediatric intensive care room with her youngest child, praying for a miracle. We were all praying for a miracle, even as we helped with funeral arrangements for the poor young father who had suffered from a depression that neither his family's love nor medicine could lift.

Two days after the suicide, while my husband and our little houseguest drove to the airport to pick up her grandparents, I went to the hospital to see her mother and sister. While I was there, something strange happened. All night long, the poor tired mother had refused to leave her child alone in the room, not wanting her to wake up and find herself among strangers. So when I arrived, I volunteered to sit with the little girl while her mother washed up and had a rest. She thanked me with tears in her eyes and then went out into the hallway to ask the nursing staff where she could wash up and lie down for a few minutes.

I sat down in the chair by the bed, looking sadly at the sweet face of the tiny little girl sleeping her life away. This is not your fault, I told myself, though I did not believe it. I could hear the mother talking outside to the nurse as I sat there, watching the little girl breathe in and out, in and out. Suddenly, the temperature in the room dropped about twenty degrees. I shivered in the sudden cold, rubbing my arms to warm them. And then I was aware of an invisible presence entering the room. Footsteps came toward me, though I could see no one approach, and I felt someone walk past me. The invisible person actually bumped against my chair, shifting it forward a few inches. I heard the footsteps walk to the side of the bed and saw the dark hair on the little girl's head flatten as if a hand was patting it. The invisible hand swept a strand of hair off the child's cheek, and I heard a man's voice speaking words

DADDY'S VISIT

I couldn't understand. Then the presence was gone as suddenly as it had come. And in that instant the child's eyes popped open, and she sat up in bed.

I exclaimed in surprise, and my neighbor came running into the room with the nurse. And the little child who—it was supposed—would never speak again called out to her mother in a perfectly rational voice: "Mama! Mama!"

It was a miracle. There was no other word for it. The little girl held out her tiny arms, and her mother swept her up into a huge hug. The child hugged her back and said, "Daddy was here. He said he was sorry I had gotten hurt and that he missed me."

I swallowed hard when I heard her words. Was it her father I had just felt in the room with us?

The child continued: "Daddy told me I was going to be all right and that it was time for me to wake up. So I did."

I gasped. So did the nurse. My neighbor was crying—tears of joy for her daughter's recovery and of pain for the loss of her husband. As the nurse checked over her patient, I tiptoed quietly out of the room and left them alone. A great weight had rolled off my shoulders when the little girl awoke. The guilt I had felt at not reporting the running car sooner was gone now that she was awake and acting herself. Somehow, I knew everything was going to be all right. And it was all tied somehow to the visit from her father's ghost. He had not wanted his daughter to suffer because of his mistake, and he had come back to make things right.

I shivered a bit, spooked by the thought even as I was grateful for its result. Then I went to phone my husband with the good news.

3

The Nightmare

OCRACOKE

The nightmare began almost as soon as I shut my eyes. I found myself crouching behind a water barrel on the deck of the *Ranger*, watching in heart-pounding fear as pirates swarmed aboard the ship. Seven, eight, nine, ten I counted. And the eleventh . . . My heart seemed to lodge itself in my throat, and I choked, clapping a hand over my mouth to keep the buccaneers from hearing me. He had a long beard that nearly covered his face. Tall and striking in appearance, the pirate wore a crimson coat with two bandoliers full of pistols and knives crossed on his chest, and two sharp swords at his waist. It was Blackbeard! A couple of cannon fuses stuck out from under his hat in my dream—something that hadn't happened in real life. They were hissing and spitting out smoke, creating such a terrifying aspect that I cowered, even in hiding.

Below decks, the hold was full of sailors waiting for this moment, but even that knowledge did not stop my heart from pounding in fear as the pirates spread out on the empty deck, their eyes searching for any sign of the crew. I screwed up my courage as best I could, waiting for the signal to attack. When it came, soldiers erupted from everywhere with shouts and loud battle cries.

I leapt out from behind the barrel and charged into the fray, finding myself only a few feet from the mighty pirate captain. Blackbeard whirled to face me, his eyes alight with joy in the fight. He was huge, much taller than I and so fierce that my whole body trembled at the sight of him. I aimed my gun with shaking hands and stepped back a pace to regain my balance against a slight swell moving the ship. My foot landed on a rope instead of the flat boards of the deck. I stumbled, couldn't regain my balance, fell . . .

. . . And woke with my heart pounding so hard that it hurt my chest. In my head, the pirate's fierce black eyes still pierced through mine, and his pistol was raised to shoot me dead where I lay.

I was sweating like a pig under the blankets. My camp bed creaked as I turned over and fumbled for the lantern with shaking hands. It was three months later, and I still could not get that horrible moment out of my mind. We'd won the battle. We'd won. A shout from Lieutenant Maynard had distracted Blackbeard at the critical moment, turning him to face his arch enemy and giving me time to roll away to safety. I was back on my feet in time to see the two mighty men engage in battle. Yet in spite of my happy ending, the Blackbeard nightmare persisted. I knew he was dead. I'd ridden home on a ship with Blackbeard's severed head displayed prominently on the bow, and yet somehow . . .

Somehow, my mind refused to believe that the pirate was really dead. I kept reliving that fateful moment again and again. The skirmish had been over in a flash—just a few seconds of my life. But in my dream, every terrifying moment happened in slow motion. I saw again every minute expression on the pirate's face as he prepared to kill me. I felt my fingers gripping the gun, felt the slip of my foot on the rough rope, felt every motion as my body went down onto the deck. I thought I was dead. I would have been, had it not been for Maynard.

In the end, it was the nightmare that had brought me back to the Carolinas, to this small island of Ocracoke. I had heard reports from my fellow officers that the ghost of Blackbeard had been seen on the shores of the Pamlico Sound. He carried a lantern in his hand and searched the beaches for his lost head. It was just the sort of superstitious nonsense that always arose after a major battle. But this time I wanted to see for myself whether it was really true. I had nothing else to do. The nightmares were affecting my health so badly now that I'd been sent home on medical leave. Perhaps, I reasoned, if I saw the ghost of the pirate that haunted my dreams, my mind would finally be convinced that he was dead, and the nightmares would cease. Anyway, it was worth a try. So I sailed out to the island with a small tent, a camp bed, and provisions. And now here I was, awakened again by the nightmare, just in time to go out along the shores of the sound and watch for a ghost that probably did not exist.

With a sigh I rolled out of bed, dressed myself warmly against the sea winds, and went to sit on the dunes near my tiny fire. A million stars wheeled over my head as I gazed quietly upward. A wisp of a moon was already low on the horizon, getting ready to set. I listened to the swish of the wind in the long grasses, the lapping of the waves in the sound. Somewhere close, crickets chirped and night creatures hunted. It was peaceful and soothing, a far cry from my nightmare. I really wasn't expecting to see anything as I pulled a blanket around my shoulders and deeply breathed the fresh air.

I don't know how long I was sitting there in a half-doze when I realized that one of the stars low on the horizon was moving toward me. I blinked in confusion and watched it for a while. Then I realized I was seeing a lantern. Someone holding a lantern was strolling up from the beach. Pulse pounding, I wondered, *Is it Blackbeard?* Then common sense reasserted itself. It couldn't be. Okay, maybe I'd come here to see a ghost. But in reality, I didn't believe that ghosts existed. And even if I did, they certainly never appeared on command (they are a lot like children in that respect). I certainly wasn't expecting a ghost sighting on the first night of my stay.

In spite of these reassuring thoughts, my body was sweating with fear as the footsteps approached. Then I made out the face of one of the local fishermen, lit by the lantern, and I had to chuckle at myself. Relieved (and a little disappointed), I called a greeting. He came up to me, and we shook hands. He was out night fishing and had come to my campsite to issue me an invitation to join his family for Sunday dinner—which was scheduled for noon the next day. I accepted the invitation gratefully. A hot, home-cooked meal was always welcome to a traveler. We sat for a couple of minutes talking about this and that before he made his way back to his fishing boat. I walked down to the boat with him and bade him good fishing. Then I watched him row out into the sound, his lantern a bobbing light that faded slowly into the night.

I stood for a while, letting my eyes adjust to the darkness. Then I turned and walked slowly back toward my camp, smiling a little at the supernatural fear I'd felt at the sight of that lantern. Suddenly, I accidentally bumped into someone passing me in the dark. "I beg your pardon," I said automatically as I stepped aside for the person to pass.

17

"Watch where yer walking," a voice grumbled back from the darkness, and I felt the swish of a large body pressing close to mine. I froze suddenly in mind-numbing fear. I was standing on a wide-open, empty beach under the glimmering starlight. How could I have bumped into someone? I was the only one there. And yet I heard the crunch of footsteps on the sand behind me, as that someone kept walking. Swallowing hard, I turned around—and saw nothing but empty beach and the wide darkness of the water, glimmering softly in the starlight.

Then a blue light glowed suddenly, as if the cover on a dark lantern had been lifted. It blinded my eyes with its dazzle. I lifted a hand to shield my gaze and caught a glimpse of a crimson coat with two bandoliers full of pistols and knives crossed on a broad chest, and two sharp swords at a thin waist. But I saw no bushy black beard. The phantom had no head at all. Just a bloody stump where its head should be.

"My head . . . Where's my head?" The glowing blue figure howled the words aloud, its voice a heart-wrenching shriek in the darkness. How it could speak without a mouth I would never know. Nor did I care to find out.

My feet were much smarter than my brain. They had me heading up the dunes toward my fire and my tent while my head was still turned back toward the beach, staring at the ghost. The phantom vanished suddenly with a popping sound. I gave a shriek that would have shamed a banshee and dove headfirst through the door of my tent. I huddled for a long time under my camp bed before, shamefaced, I crept into it and went to sleep. After all, I reasoned as my shaking slowly ceased, I had come here to see a ghost. I shouldn't act like such a coward when it actually happened.

THE NIGHTMARE

That night, for the first time since the battle, I slept without dreams. And when I awoke, I knew I was cured. At least of the first nightmare! I wasn't sure how I was going to cure myself of the vision of the ghost. I shook like a frightened child whenever I recalled it.

Completely overcome by my Blackbeard sighting, I packed up my belongings as soon as I awoke and loaded them into my small sailing skiff. Then I spent the morning fishing as far away from the haunted beach as I could go and still keep my promise to have dinner with the fisherman and his family at noon. It was a wonderful meal, and I heartily wished I had been able to enjoy it. But every mouthful tasted like sawdust to me, so deep was my longing to get away from the island.

As soon as common courtesy would allow, I bade farewell to my host and hostess and sailed away from the haunted dunes overlooking the Pamlico Sound, never to return there during the length of my days. I did not want to risk having a third encounter with the legendary pirate. Two meetings were more than enough!

4

Ghost Light

MACO

I thought the kids would get a big kick out of it when I suggested we stop on the way to the seashore to watch for the Maco Light. After all, kids like spooky stuff. But they were dubious about the proposition, and my wife, Amanda, was downright skeptical.

"Why do you want to watch for some old ghost light?" she complained. "I thought you didn't believe in that stuff."

"I'm a skeptic. Seeing is believing," I replied.

The kids chimed in then. My daughter, Lily, was eager to see the ghost light, but Kevin Junior just wanted to get to the beach.

"We won't get there till after dark anyway. You won't be able to go to the beach until tomorrow," I said firmly. And that was that. Kev rolled his eyes expressively at my authoritarian manner and then subsided into a sulk in the backseat. Teenagers! When I complained to my own father about my teenager, he laughed at me and told me my mother had wished him on me. Apparently, I was just the same when I was a kid.

It was dusk by the time we neared our destination. I switched on the car headlights and turned down the road toward Maco.

To get the kids in the mood, I told them the story of the Maco Light in my best spooky manner.

There was once a railroad conductor named Joe Baldwin who was working for the newly rebuilt Atlantic Coast Line. The year was 1867, and the railroad had expanded to include a small station in Maco, North Carolina. Joe was assigned to the very last car in the train, and he executed his conductor duties to the best of his abilities aboard his assigned car. Then one night, something went wrong. Terribly wrong. The train was heading down the line toward the tiny Maco station when Joe's car started to slow down dramatically. Worried, Joe went forward to see what was happening, and he realized that his car had become decoupled from the rest of the train. Joe's heart leapt into his throat when he saw the retreating lights of the train disappearing into the distance. His car was stuck on the tracks, and another train was following close behind them.

With a shout of dismay, Joe grabbed his signal lantern and frantically ran the length of the car. Bursting out of the back door, he ran out onto the rear platform. Yes, he could see the next train speeding toward them down the track. By the look of it, the engineer had not realized the danger. Joe leaned over the rail, desperately signaling for the engineer in the following train to stop. But the train barreled forward, its speed unabated. Joe realized that the engineer must not have seen his signal light— or perhaps had not realized its significance. He kept waving the lantern frantically from side to side, shouting in vain over the huge rumbling force of the oncoming train. The engine grew larger and larger, and Joe's heart was in his throat as he realized the train was not going to stop.

With a thunderous roar and the great shriek of massive metal hitting massive metal, the engine struck the helpless car. Joe, still at his post, was smashed between the two trains; his head was severed from his body. The signal lantern flew wildly out of his hand, rolling along beside the tangled metal of the two trains and miraculously flipping upright, still alight. Joe was the only fatality in the railway accident that night. The railroad officials never located his head.

Shortly after the train accident, the Maco Light began to appear on the tracks near the station. People traveling on the train, or crossing the tracks at Maco, would report a light shining in the distance when no train was due. The light would appear as a small ball, far down the tracks, and then would come closer and closer to the observer until it was the size of a lantern. People reported that the light moved back and forth frantically, as if it were signaling a train to stop, just as Joe Baldwin had done the night of the accident.

The phenomenon became so common that the Atlantic Coast Line Railroad ordered their engineers not to stop for the light if they saw it as they were approaching Maco. Folks believed it was the spirit of Joe the conductor, desperately replaying his final moments over and over again, trying to get the following train to stop before it hit his helpless car.

As I finished the story, Kevin Junior gave an annoying and rather dramatic sigh and said, "Boring." I ignored him and turned into the pull-off beside the railroad tracks. It was a dark night, and it got even darker as I shut down the engine and turned off the lights.

"My teacher said President Grover Cleveland saw the Maco Light once in 1889 when he was riding the train," Lily piped up from the backseat.

"That's right," I said enthusiastically, tossing her a happy smile over my shoulder.

We were the only ones at the pull-off that night. The moon had already set, and it was very dark. There were no vehicles passing on the lonesome highway, and all I could hear were the swish of the wind and the rattle, buzz, chirp, and bump of night creatures in the woods. I leaned back in my seat and waited, watching the faint glimmer of the railroad tracks in the starlight.

"This is boring," said Kevin after ten minutes of silence.

"Then take a nap," I suggested.

Ten more minutes passed. An owl hooted back in the woods, and Lily jumped. "What was that?" she whispered. Kevin laughed at her. "It's just a boring owl," he said.

Ten more minutes went by. "Honey, that dratted light is not going to show itself tonight," Amanda said. "Let's go."

And then a small dot of white light appeared far down the railroad tracks. My chest tightened in excitement, and my heart started to pound against my ribs. "Look at that! Look!" I said hoarsely, pointing. Everyone looked, even Kevin.

"It's just someone with a flashlight," Kevin said a bit uncertainly after a moment. We ignored him, breathlessly watching as the light moved slowly forward, getting larger and brighter as it approached.

At first I was excited to see it. Then goose bumps raised on my skin, and I began to feel a bit . . . well, creepy. There was something disconcerting about a light with no source coming closer . . . closer. Nothing was behind it or above it or below it to explain why it was there. Nothing at all. At least nothing I could see.

Ghost Light

I could feel my whole body trembling. Beside me, Amanda gripped my arm so hard it hurt. "Make it stop, Daddy. Make it stop," Lily whimpered from the backseat. The light hovered at man-height above the ground and was now the size of a lantern. Then it started frantically moving from side to side, as if it were signaling. And no one was holding it! No one at all.

My heart was hammering so heavily that it actually hurt my chest, and my throat felt so tight that I could not make a sound. Even my legs started to shake. For a moment it looked as if the light would come right into the car with us! I was reaching with trembling hands for the keys when the light vanished abruptly, just a few feet from our car.

Everyone gasped in fear and relief. Amanda loosened her grip on my arm. "Where did it go?" Lily asked at the same moment that Kevin said, "Maco Ghost Light! That was cool! Can we do it again?"

I cleared my throat a couple of times. "I think once is enough for tonight," I managed to say in a voice that sounded a few pitches too high.

"Once is enough for forever," Amanda muttered.

"Let's head to the hotel," I said in a more normal tone as I started the car and turned back onto the highway. I needed to see people milling about, streetlights that had a source, and the other trappings of normal society. The sight of that bodiless light floating toward me would haunt my dreams for quite a while, and I was not sure I wanted to see it again.

Like Amanda said, some things you do only once.

5

The Little Red Man

WINSTON-SALEM

It was amazing how these folktales sprang up, the visitor mused, accepting a cup of coffee from the serving girl. He sat back in his chair, eyeing his friend askance. Frankly, it surprised him to hear a prominent member of the Moravian Church talking about a ghost. He had not thought that the church would approve of the telling of such tales.

The town of Salem had been settled by the Moravian church in 1766, as part of the North Carolina Wachovia settlement. The Moravians were a Protestant sect with a strong missionary focus, and the church played a central role in their lives. The church strictly divided the members of its congregation by sex. Men and women sat in separate sections of the church during services and the unmarried men and women in the church were divided into "Choirs" (groups classified according to age and sex). Several houses were created to care for the spiritual and temporal welfare of the Choirs. These included the Houses of Single Brethren, Single Sisters, and Widows. It was only after a marriage took place that families were allowed to live together under one roof.

27

According to his friend—one of the more prominent citizens in Salem—it was one of these Houses that had become famed for its ghost. Its ghost! How ridiculous.

"It really is a most interesting tale," the Salem citizen mused, taking a sip of coffee from his cup.

The visitor raised a skeptical eyebrow at him.

The Salem citizen laughed: "I know you don't believe in ghosts, *mein Freund,* but listen to the tale yourself, and then decide!" He went on to relate the ghostly tale in full.

Brother Andreas Kramer was a single man working as a shoemaker and living in the Single Brothers' dormitory in town. He was a happy little man who walked the streets of Salem with his red cap perched jauntily on his head. He would nod cheerfully to everyone he met, and the children in town all loved him for his playful spirit and good heart.

One evening in March, Brother Kramer—who had been uncommonly quiet all day—joined a few of his brothers in the excavation of the new cellar for the extension to the Single Brothers' house after attending the evening services. The men were cutting into the earthen bank and then pulling down the overhang. It was an excavation technique that had been successfully used in the past, but some brothers doubted the wisdom of using it for this particular cellar, because of the sandy nature of the soil.

However, the brothers who objected to this method were overruled by the majority, and thus it was that Brother Kramer and several other men were kneeling under the overhanging bank when it collapsed. The other men made it out safely, but Andreas was buried. Frantically, the men dug into the cave-in, trying to rescue their friend. A hint of red cloth became visible in the lantern light, guiding their digging. A few moments later, the owner of the red cap was visible underneath the dirt and debris that had buried him. But when the poor shoemaker was gently pulled out of the rubble, it was obvious that he was dying. One leg was twisted and broken, and he seemed to be suffering from internal injuries as well. The cave-in happened at midnight, and by 2:00 a.m. the shoemaker was dead.

Every member of the Moravian Church was saddened by the loss of the cheerful little man in the red cap. What they didn't expect was the sudden flurry of supernatural activity in the Single Brothers' house after the death of Andreas the shoemaker. The men digging out the cellar and building the new addition often sensed the presence of someone working beside them, even when they were quite alone. The tap-tap-tap sound of the shoemaker working in his dorm room still rang through the building occasionally, making the Single Brothers smile. And every once in a while, the men would hear the patter of footsteps, just before a partially transparent little man in a red cap slipped past an open doorway and vanished down the hallway.

Pausing to take another sip of coffee, the Salem man grinned at his visitor. "Would you like to hear more?" he asked. Gruffly, pretending disinterest, the visitor nodded and beckoned to the serving girl to refill his coffee cup.

After a time, the Salem citizen continued, the haunted house was no longer needed for the Single Brothers, so it became a home for several families to share and eventually became a home for widows. The widows liked to giggle and gossip about the little red-capped fellow they sometimes saw in the hallway. One time, when a little deaf girl came for a visit to her granny, the child asked the old woman about the "funny little red man" whom she had seen several times in and around the house. The old woman was astonished. Her granddaughter had lost her hearing as a tiny child and knew nothing of the story of Brother Kramer, yet here she was asking about the ghost as if she had really seen him!

The Salem citizen paused again and grinned at the visitor. "Pretty strong evidence, that!"

The visitor snorted. "If you like," he grunted in disbelief.

"Well, then, let us pay a visit to the house," the Salem man said with a smile. "You are a builder by trade, and the house has some very interesting subcellars you might be interested in viewing, including the one that was instrumental in that fatal accident so long ago. And who knows, we may even catch a glimpse of a red cap!"

The visitor chuckled in polite disbelief but acceded to the plan. Permission from the widows was quickly granted, and the two men went down to the sub-basement level. The visitor was soon absorbed in the architecture of the place, asking interested questions about the excavation and construction of the building.

When they reached the fatal cellar, the Salem man pointed to the place where the collapse had happened and reiterated the story of the little Red Man. The visitor gave a polite snort, turned, and then froze in place with a gasp. The temperature in the air around the men dropped more than twenty degrees in a second, and before their eyes was a small, wiry man wearing a red cap. His feet were a good six inches above the floor of the cellar, and he folded his arms and mimicked the visitor's disbelieving frown to perfection.

THE LITTLE RED MAN

The visitor felt his flesh creep in reaction to this strange visitation, but he was a brave man and forced himself to move forward toward the apparition. "Let's see if you're really real," he said in a voice that was just a shade higher than his normal pitch. The visitor lunged at him and stepped right through his body. It felt like being stabbed by a thousand icicles all at once. The visitor gasped and bent over for a second against the horrible sensation that was almost painful in its intensity. When he recovered a bit, he glanced back over his shoulder.

"I told you," the Salem man said from behind him. The Salem man hadn't moved a muscle when the ghost appeared. He was sweating a little but wore a half-smile too. The visitor frowned at him. "Somebody's playing a trick on us," he said. "I just can't figure out how they made the feet appear as if they didn't touch the ground."

"If you like," the Salem man said in polite skepticism.

There came a tap-tap-tap from the doorway. The visitor whirled around. The little Red Man hovered in the doorway, grinning from ear to ear, and happily saluted the visitor from the doorway. His feet still did not touch the ground. Then he vanished with a small popping noise.

The visitor's eyes met those of the Salem man. They stared at each other for a long moment—the one ashen, the other smiling.

"All right," the visitor said at last. "I will grant you a ghost. Now let's get out of here!"

The Salem man laughed. Then he took the visitor away to the tavern and offered him a drink to sooth his jangled nerves.

Their encounter with the ghost became a favorite story of the Salem citizens in later years, even after a visiting minister laid the ghost to rest. The Salem man wasn't sure if he should be happy or sorry that the ghost was gone. Still, it made a fair tale, even from the far side of the vale.

6

Phantom Horseman

GREENSBORO

Some things you just don't anticipate. I didn't anticipate finding myself homeless after the divorce. But somehow, my ex-wife ended up with the house and the car, and I ended up homeless with a golden retriever to feed.

After a bit of fancy footwork, I got a small place in Greensboro near a local park, which had some good walking paths. Jeeter and I jogged together every day, and our new neighborhood, with its easy access to the park, was a wonderful place to do it. Shortly after moving in, I learned that the park and all of the area surrounding it—including my house—had been the site of a Revolutionary War battlefield. Unfamiliar with the story, I did some digging at the local library to learn more and was intrigued to discover that my property had some historical significance.

The Battle of Guilford Courthouse took place between the British troops, led by Major General Lord Cornwallis, and the Continental Army, led by Major General Nathanael Greene. According to the history books, Cornwallis was chasing the Continental Army through the Carolinas, trying to defeat them. Greene stayed well ahead but chose this particular vicinity to make his stand. He set up three battle lines, and Cornwallis rushed to attack him on the morning of March 15, 1781, by which time his troops were hungry and tired. The British advanced up a road through thickly wooded country to an area cleared for grazing, where they engaged the first of three lines of American soldiers. The British broke through all three lines after heavy fighting on both sides and sent the Continental Army into retreat, although the casualties inflicted on the British made it more of a defeat for them than a decisive victory.

I told the story to Jeeter during our jog the morning after I'd done my research. Jeeter was not impressed. I guess he would prefer to live on a battlefield where the American troops had defeated the British. Still, as I told him, Greene's men had harassed Cornwallis's army so badly that they never recovered, and shortly thereafter they were defeated at Yorktown—ending the Revolutionary War in our favor.

We'd been in our new home for three months when Jeeter brought me the leash one evening, wagging his golden tail enthusiastically. We'd jogged already that morning, but he wanted to go out again. Since I had no big plans for the evening, a walk seemed like a pleasant idea. We wandered down the street as we listened to the soft chirping of crickets and the call of night birds from the dark trees in the park, which backed all the houses on the street. It was a lovely warm evening, strangely bereft of human company. The houses on either side of us were silent and dark, and the soft whistle of the wind was the only noise aside from the rustle of night creatures in the park.

Abruptly, Jeeter stopped walking. The hair bristled up all along his back, and he growled. I glanced ahead, following his gaze. A shadowy figure had appeared on the darkened street between the pools of light that came from the lampposts. I heard a clip-clop, clip-clop noise coming toward me. It sounded like hoofbeats—a strange thing to hear in this modern place. Was someone riding a horse toward us?

Jeeter's tail clamped suddenly between his back legs. He gave a whimper of fright and cowered behind me, tangling me up in his leash so tightly that I couldn't move. I just stood there, watching a dark figure approaching me on horseback while my dog trembled against my legs. The horseman rode under a streetlight, and I saw him clearly for the first time. He must have been doing a historical gig for one of the local schools, because he was dressed in the uniform of a Continental soldier. He had his part down perfectly, looking about as tattered and weary and heartsore as any man might who was part of a defeated army.

"Good eve, young sir," the man called to me.

"Good evening," I replied cautiously. The breeze arose around us. Now it felt cold on my skin, and I shivered, my arms suddenly prickly with goose bumps. I was filled with the strong desire to flee to the safety of my own house. I dismissed this ridiculous notion as the horseman reined in his beast beside me. He sat looking at me in silence for a moment. It was uncanny. I felt as if I were caught up in a strange tableau, or a painting of some kind. I was frozen in place and could do nothing to remove myself from this encounter.

Jeeter whined against the back of my tangled legs. I felt my heart pounding and my flesh crawling under the soldier's stare.

"This place, these houses," the soldier said finally, gesturing with the whip in his hand. He seemed to be pointing directly at my house, even though it was several yards down from our present location. "They have been built on the bodies of the slain."

I glanced around me. I had never thought of that. I supposed it must be true. Many people had died in this place during the battle.

I nodded. "I believe you are right," I said cautiously, absently stroking my dog's head, as much to comfort myself as to comfort him.

The horseman looked me straight in the eye. Under the streetlight, he appeared pale, almost ethereal, as if he were not quite real. "It is not good to desecrate this place. Do not disturb the dead," he said sternly. And he vanished.

Jeeter trembled violently against my legs. I gave a yelp of surprise and felt the spell that had paralyzed me evaporate suddenly. I turned abruptly, forgetting the tangled leash, and fell over Jeeter. For a moment all was tangled leash, sweaty dog, and swearing owner. Then we were both on our feet and running for home in great leaps and bounds. Jeeter beat me to the front door by a hair's breadth and whined at me while my shaking hands fumbled with lock and key. We stumbled inside, and I slammed the door behind us and leaned against it.

"A ghost," I gasped aloud. "That man was a ghost." I glanced around for Jeeter, but my dog had vanished. I found him later, cowering under the bed.

I kept waking up that night, cold shudders running across my skin, hearing the phantom's final words over and over in my mind: "Do not disturb the dead."

I rose in the morning heavy-eyed and unready for the morning jog. Jeeter, who normally woke me with leash in mouth and tail wagging, was visibly absent. He was still under the bed and refused to come out.

Phantom Horseman

I left for work without going for a jog and jumped every time someone spoke to me at the office. When I got home, Jeeter was still under the bed. That decided me. I went to the closet, pulled out a suitcase, and began packing. "We're getting out of here," I told my dog.

Jeeter must have understood. As soon as I was packed, he crept out from under the bed with his leash in his mouth and trotted to the back door. I hauled the suitcase after him, and a minute later we drove away from that haunted neighborhood and didn't look back. I hired movers to pack up my place—I had nightmares just thinking about setting foot in that house again—and settled over in Winston-Salem with my dog.

7

I'm So Cold

DARE COUNTY

Mary and Kate were two sisters who were very close for kinfolk. They married two brothers and lived on the same street in the same little town, and their kids always played together. It was something to see. Not many folks get along so well with their kin!

But Mary had a secret that no one knew about—not even Kate. 'Specially not Kate. You see, Mary was jealous of Kate's man. Not that she wanted him for herself. No, what she wanted was the money he brought home to Kate. The brother Mary married wasn't good with finances, and Mary's clothes and shoes and house weren't half as nice as Kate's.

All this jealousy, in the end, focused on one item. Mary became obsessed with the fancy diamond ring her brother-in-law put on his wife's hand the day they married. Sometimes, she'd stare at her sister's hand when Kate was busy with her little son—who was an only child, and once she asked to try on the diamond ring, which fit Mary perfectly. But other than that, Mary didn't talk about her obsession. After all, Kate and her husband were generous, and they bought Mary and her young daughters' gifts all the time.

Still, the jealousy festered in Mary through the years as her daughters grew up and left home. Then Mary's husband died, followed shortly by Kate's man, and the two sisters moved in together for company. And that's when things got bad. Mary started making nasty remarks about Kate having money. Kate was shocked. Here she was, thinking Mary loved her unconditionally, and her sister had fooled her all these years. Kate was so hurt, she moved out of the house the very next morning and didn't come back.

So Mary lived all alone in her little house, growing meaner and more cross every day. Mary didn't see anyone for days on end but the grocer boy and the milkman. Her daughters lived far away and rarely visited. When they did phone, Mary tried to poison their minds against their Aunt Kate, saying that she'd left Mary to fend all alone and went to live the posh life with her son in Raleigh.

When the nephew called to tell Mary that Kate had passed, he didn't know anything about a quarrel between the sisters. Mary felt a pang about that in the region where her heart was supposed to be. Here she was, thinking Kate had poisoned her nephew against his aunty, and it wasn't so.

Mary had done a much better job turning her girls against Kate. Her daughters refused to attend their aunt's funeral, but Mary dropped everything and went all the way to Raleigh to assist her nephew with the arrangements. She helped lay out the body and picked out Kate's nicest outfit to dress her in. And Mary took the diamond ring off Kate's finger when her nephew wasn't looking, figuring Kate didn't need it anymore.

They buried Kate the next morning, and Mary went back to her little house to gloat over her diamond ring. And not just the diamond ring. According to her nephew, Kate had laid by a tidy sum just for her sister. Mary felt bad about that, but not enough to stop her enjoying the new ring. She loved to watch it sparkle on her hand.

One night, Mary woke suddenly in her dark bedroom, sure she'd heard someone call her name. She blinked up at the ceiling, realizing that there was a glow coming from her doorway. She rolled over, wondering if one of her daughters had come in the night without phoning her first. But it wasn't her daughter. Floating in the hallway, outlined by the frame of the open doorway was a glowing blue figure. "Mary," it called. "Mary! I'm c-c-cold, Mary!"

Mary's heart started banging against her chest, and she broke out into a cold sweat. She knew that voice. She hadn't heard it since the day of the argument, but she recognized it. The blue figure was the ghost of Kate.

Mary rolled over quickly and pulled the covers over her head, pretending she didn't hear anything. "Go away, ghost," she muttered. "Go away. I don't have anything of yours." She felt a swirling breeze brush her fingertips where they clutched the eiderdown over her head. She pulled her fingers under the covers and waited grimly until the wind died down and the sense of a presence died with it. She checked the diamond ring to make sure it was still on her finger. Then she went to sleep.

It was the breeze that woke Mary the next night. Outside in the hall, a groaning sound began: "Ooooooooo! Oooooooo! Mary! Mary!"

A blue figure hovered in the doorway, changing shades rapidly from white to sky blue to dark blue and back again, over and over. The strobing pattern made the shadows in the room flicker harshly, giving Mary a headache. She shuddered with chills and clutched the eiderdown close to her, the diamond ring sparkling in the changing blue light.

"Mary! I'm c-c-cold, Mary!" the ghost of Kate wailed despairingly.

"Why are you cold?" Mary retorted, closing her eyes against the flicker.

"The grave's so cold," the ghost wailed, making Mary shiver and shake under the eiderdown.

Mary shouted: "Go away, ghost. Go away. I don't have anything of yours."

The breeze swirled around her for a minute or more, tugging at her hair, her face, her hands. She tucked the hand with the diamond ring under her armpit and grimly kept her eyes closed until the wind died down and the sense of a presence died with it. But she couldn't get back to sleep that night.

The next morning, she visited one of the local conjure women and asked how to get rid of a ghost. After she gave the conjurer a description of the ghost (though she didn't tell her about the diamond ring), the woman told her to ask the ghost to come into the room to get warm. Mary nodded thoughtfully. Yes, maybe that would do the trick. Once Kate warmed up, she'd forget all about haunting her sister.

That night, when Mary felt the cold breeze swirl through her room, she sat up in bed right away. Sure enough, a glowing blue figure materialized in the doorway.

"Mary! I'm c-c-cold, Mary," the ghost of Kate wailed despairingly.

"Come in, ghost, and get warm," Mary said, speaking as calmly as she could against the terrified lump in her throat.

I'm So Cold

Her whole body was shaking like a tree in a windstorm as the blue figure floated closer and closer to the bed. It moved in a funny way, jerking this way and that like a puppet on a string. It seemed to be looking for something. Mary's heart pounded so hard her ribs hurt. She knew what the ghost was looking for.

"Why'd you come here, ghost?" she said, teeth chattering from fright.

"I'm loooookin' fer soooomething," the ghost wailed, jerking its glowing blue head back and forth.

"What are you looking for?" asked Mary. The guilty question slipped out of her mouth afore she could stop it.

"My riiiiiinnngg! I want my ring!" the ghost of Kate wailed, its voice rising so high only hound dogs could hear the top notes. The pressure on Mary's ears was something awful. She clapped both hands over her ears and shouted: "I ain't got it!"

"Yes, you *do!*" roared the ghost.

Mary felt a wrenching pain in her hand, and then breeze, light, ghost, and sound vanished. Taking Mary's finger and the diamond ring with it.

Mary fainted and didn't wake up till morning. In the bright sunlight beaming onto her bed, she saw that her finger was gone! A cauterized stump was all that remained.

Mary never explained to her daughters how she lost her ring finger. But she never stole anything again. She learned her lesson at last.

8

The Handshake

GOLDSBORO

Polly was the sweetest, prettiest girl in Goldsboro, yes sir. All the local boys were chasing her, and quite a number of the fellows from the surrounding countryside were too. All the girls were jealous of Polly 'cause they didn't have no sweethearts to take them to the local dances, but even they couldn't help liking her. Polly would give someone the shirt off her back if they needed it. That's just the way she was. Of course, the girls all wanted Polly to choose her man so things could go back to normal. But Polly was picky. None of the local boys suited her, and neither did the fellows from the backcountry.

Then one day, George Dean came home from university, and Polly was smitten. He was handsome, tall, and mysterious. He didn't chase her like the other fellows. He seemed to favor the other girls. For weeks Polly fumed as George played beau to first one pretty girl then another. Didn't he see her at all? She was in a real tizzy by the time handsome George Dean wandered up to her front porch one evening and asked if she'd care to take a stroll down the lane. Polly sniffed and acted haughty at first, but finally she allowed that a stroll might not come amiss.

From that moment on, Polly and George were inseparable. You couldn't turn around without bumping into them at one social event or another. Polly completely dropped all her other beaus, much to the relief of the local girls, and soon the town was filled with the laughter of many courting couples. The Saturday night dances were particularly popular, and it was at one of those that George proposed, and Polly accepted. There was great rejoicing—particularly among the eligible young females, who'd been afeared of what might happen if Polly broke it off with George.

A day was set, and Polly started making preparations for the wedding and shopping for items to fill her new home. George wasn't too interested in all the fripperies and wedding details. He left the womenfolk to get on with it and started spending time down at the pool hall with some of his buddies. And that's where he met Helene, the owner's saucy daughter. She had bold black eyes and ruby-red lips, and a bad-girl air that fascinated George. He spent more and more time at the pool hall, and less and less time with Polly, who finally noticed in spite of all the hustle and bustle.

She made a few inquiries, and Cindy—a girl who'd lost her favorite beau to Polly a few years back—told her *all about* Helene. In detail.

Of course, Polly was furious. She immediately confronted George with the story, and he couldn't deny it. Suddenly, George had to toe the mark. His pool-hall visits were over, and he spent every free hour he wasn't at work by her side. That didn't sit well with George, but his family backed Polly up, so he went along with it.

The day of the wedding dawned clear and bright. Polly and her bridesmaids went to the church to get dressed in their finery, whispering excitedly together. The guests filled the sanctuary, and the pastor and the best man waited patiently in the antechamber for the groom's arrival. They waited. And waited. And waited some more. But George didn't come.

The best man hurried into the sanctuary to talk to the groom's father, who hustled back to the house right quick to check on his son. Still no George. Had he been in an accident? Was he hurt? No one knew the answer.

George's brothers went searching for him, calling in at the police, at the hospital. His youngest brother even went to the pool hall. And that's when he found out that Helene was missing too. Helene's youngest sister told George's youngest brother that she'd seen them leave the pool hall together about an hour before the wedding. So that was that.

With dread, Polly's mother went to tell her daughter what had happened. Polly, all bright and shining and lovely in her long white dress and soft wedding veil, turned pale when her mother broke the news.

"It couldn't be. George would never do that!" she exclaimed. She stared blankly at her mother, swayed a bit, and then stiffened, grabbing her left arm as a sudden pain ripped through it. She was dead from a massive heart attack before she hit the floor.

And so Polly's wedding became—in essence—Polly's wake. Her family was furious. George's family was furious and embarrassed. And the guests were furious too. George's unthinking actions had killed the sweetest, prettiest girl in Goldsboro. If he was going to jilt her, the gossips all agreed, he should have done it privately. He shouldn't have left her at the altar.

A few days later Polly was buried in the churchyard, still wearing her white wedding dress and veil. The whole town came to the funeral and wept at the passing of such a beautiful young girl. George and Helene, who had spent the week happily honeymooning in the Outer Banks, arrived home at the very moment that the black-clad crowd exited the churchyard. Their arrival caused a commotion. The minister had to pull Polly's father off George before he killed him. And George's family disowned him right there in the street in front of everyone. Even the attorneys at the law office where George worked turned him away, knowing that no one in town would do business with them as long as George remained on their staff.

Helene's family was equally embarrassed. No one was visiting the pool hall anymore, and it looked like they would have to move away from town. They refused to open their door to their daughter and her new husband. Only Helene's youngest sister relented enough to open the upper window of the pool hall and speak to her sister. She dropped a bundle of clothes down to Helene and then slammed the window shut immediately afterward to make her position clear. So George and Helene left town in disgrace to make a new life for themselves elsewhere.

Life moved on. The scandal grew cold, and new ones took its place as new interests arose among the young people and the gossips. Polly and George and Helene were forgotten. Then, a year after Polly's death, George's father passed and was buried in the local churchyard just a few plots away from the girl who had almost become his daughter-in-law. This event triggered gossip about the fatal wedding day. For a few days the story of Polly and George was revived and much discussed.

Everyone in town turned out for the funeral of the elder Mr. Dean. Everyone was waiting to see if George would show his face. But George was too clever for them. He waited at an inn outside of town until it was dark, and then he went to the churchyard to pay his last respects to his father.

George Junior stood by the freshly dug grave and told his father that things weren't going so well. His old law firm had refused to give him a reference, and word of Polly's death had reached those at his former university who might have once helped him. So he was working as a farmhand, barely able to feed and clothe himself and his wife, who flagrantly chased after other men.

As he unburdened himself at his father's graveside, George heard a sweet female voice calling his name. "George. Sweetheart." George looked up in sudden hope. Was that his mother, come to forgive him? But no, the voice was pitched too high to be his mother, who sang contralto in the church choir.

"George," the voice called again. Puzzled, George turned toward the sound. And then he saw, rising up from a grassy mound under a spreading oak tree, a figure in a long white gown and a soft veil. Her eyes and her lips were yellow flames beneath the veil, and the rotted wedding dress glowed with a white-yellow light. It was Polly.

George's body stiffened, shudders of fear coursing up and down his arms and legs. Every hair on his neck prickled, and bile rose up into his throat until he retched and threw up on his father's grave. He put a shaking hand to his mouth and staggered backward, the other hand outstretched to ward off the specter floating toward him.

The spectral bride cackled with angry laughter and swooped forward until her hand closed over George's outstretched one in a terrible parody of a handshake. The grip of the spectral bride was so cold that it burned the skin, and so hard that the bones crunched as she squeezed. "Come along into the church, George," the glowing bride whispered. Through the veil, George could see maggots crawling in and out of Polly's flaming eye sockets.

"Nooo! Polly, no!" George screamed in terror, but he could not wrench his hand free. The ghost dragged him step by halting step toward the front door of the church. His hand was a red-hot agony of pain, though the rest of his body was shaking with cold. The agony was spreading now, up his arm to his shoulder.

"No!" George gave a final cry of despair and wrenched again at his hand. And suddenly, he was free. The spectral bride gave a roar of rage as George ran pell-mell down the church lane and out into the street.

"You're mine, George Dean! If not in this world, then in the next," the spectral bride howled after him. Her glowing form swelled upward until it was taller than the treetops. George looked back once and fell headlong when he saw the massive form with its flaming yellow eyes and lips and the moldering rags of its white wedding dress. He picked himself up, terror lending him speed. Clutching his aching hand, he ran all the way back to the inn.

By the time George reached his room, the fiery pain in his hand and arm was seeping through his entire body. He rang desperately for the housemaid and begged her to send for a

THE HANDSHAKE

doctor. Then he fell into bed and stared at his hand, which was black and withered, as if it had been scorched long ago by a fire. Black and red streaks were climbing up his arm so fast that he could almost see them move.

George was unconscious when the doctor arrived, and the swelling was already extending into his chest and neck. There was nothing the physician could do. The injury was too severe and had spread too far. Within two days George was dead. Polly had gotten her man at last.

9

Robah

WINSTON-SALEM

When my boyfriend, Fred, and our friends Mike and Carrie suggested partying in the graveyard one Halloween night, I said, "Why not?" That seemed a suitably spooky thing to do. It was a cloudy night, with a great deal of wind rustling and shrieking through the trees. The wind whipped leaves and debris through the air, and great blasts of it would rattle the gravestones, which made me and Carrie shriek even worse than the wind. I wasn't really scared. What I really wanted was to have Fred put his arm around me, and, by golly, it worked! Fred got all manly and protective, saying that no ghost dared mess with his girl while he was around.

"You hear me, ghosts!" he called aloud. "Don't mess with my girl!"

I lapped it up, snuggling contentedly against his side. But our friend Mike was dubious.

"I wouldn't say things like that in a graveyard," he said to Fred, shaking his head in the beam of the flashlight. "That's asking for trouble."

"Don't be silly. And come sit down here under this big gravestone," Carrie called to us. "It's kind of cozy in this spot, and it's out of the wind."

54

We looked around and saw that she'd put a blanket down on the ground by a big headstone and was busy pulling a bottle of wine from her backpack. We hurried over and settled cozily onto the blanket. It was almost like a picnic. Well, okay—make that a grisly picnic under a lowering black sky with a fierce wind whipping debris all over the place and hulking black tombstones all around us. The only light came from our flashlights, but it didn't help at all. There was some quality about the darkness that Halloween night that swallowed all the light.

As we sat in the hollow of the hill with a few icy fingers of wind creeping over us from time to time, I finally caught my breath and had a good look around. My eyes were adjusted to the darkness, and I could see a lot more than I expected. Row upon row of tombstones lined the rolling hillside. The shapes were strange sometimes, with statues and carvings interrupting the regularity of the headstones. Here and there a tree whipped wildly in that wind. It was almost gale force in its intensity, and something about its single-minded force made me shiver. For the first time that evening, I realized how truly creepy this place was. But there was no way I would admit that to anyone. Carrie was cheerfully passing out glasses of wine, and the boys were laughing.

I accepted a glass of wine from Carrie, and in the light of the flashlight, I read the name on the tombstone behind her: "Robah Gray."

Carrie blinked at me. "What?" she asked. Then she followed my gaze to the tombstone and grinned. "Oh. How thoughtless of me. Do you mind if we sit here, Robah?" she asked politely. There was (thank goodness) no response. The boys chuckled. Fred lifted the wine bottle and asked: "Want some wine, Robah?"

Still no answer (thank God).

I decided to concentrate on the wine and the conversation and to stop looking at the windswept graveyard around me. It was freaking me out. When I tuned in again, I realized Mike was still addressing the tombstone: "Don't you get tired of being stuck in this graveyard, Robah? I would." He drank the last of his wine and gestured for Fred to give him a refill. Only a few drops came out of the bottle.

"Wow. That went fast," said Carrie.

"We should have brought two bottles," said Mike with a sigh of regret.

I shivered as a few more fingers of wind found us around Robah's grave. Fred rubbed my shoulders and arms briskly to warm them and dropped a kiss on my hair.

"Annie's freezing," he announced. "We'd better get moving before she turns into an icicle."

Carrie and Mike jumped up at once, grabbing the empty bottle and blanket so quickly that I realized I wasn't the only one made uneasy by our eerie location.

"Thanks for sharing your spot with us, Robah," I said quietly to the tombstone, feeling that it wasn't respectful to leave without some acknowledgment. Silly, I know. But that's how I felt.

"Why don't you come along with us, Robah?" added Fred jovially, flinging his arm around my shoulders. "It would be more interesting than staying in a graveyard."

"Hush, Fred," I said uneasily.

I could see Mike's and Carrie's flashlights bobbing along as they navigated their way through the headstones. They were already halfway up the hillside and hurrying toward the car as fast as they could without running.

"Come on," I said, pulling Fred away as he continued to babble nonsense to Robah's grave. A great gust of wind followed us up the hillside, nearly knocking me off my feet. Fred's hand on my arm was the only thing that saved me from a nasty fall.

We reached the car only a step or two behind Carrie and Mike, and another great gust of wind blew right into the car with us.

"Whew. Creepy!" Carrie said, glancing over the front seat to where Fred and I huddled together in back.

"What a great Halloween!" Fred said cheerfully, squeezing my hand and smiling at me. Personally, I'd have preferred to go to a party. But when Fred smiled at me like that, I lost all desire to be anywhere else. I smiled back at him and then laid my head on his shoulder and fell asleep.

It was late by the time they dropped me off at my house. The wind was still gusting something fierce in the pine trees beside the house, and I seemed to be accompanied inside by a miniature whirlwind that tugged at my coat and scarf and nearly knocked me off my feet. I staggered and then shut the door on the wind, which continued to whistle around me for a moment even after the door was closed. Then I went into the den to sit for a moment beside the embers still glowing in the fireplace. I took off my hat and coat with a sigh of relief, happy to be home.

For some reason I thought of poor Robah, lying under the cold earth in the graveyard. I bet he—or was it she?—would like to be here right now! The thought made me shiver, in spite of the warmth from the fire. And when the wind gusted against the window so fiercely that the pane shook, I jumped and whirled in fright.

Enough was enough, I scolded myself, and went upstairs to bed. I was done with creepy things for one night. Well, not quite. The TV in the family room turned itself on in the middle of the night at top volume. Scared the whole family. Dad was furious—thought it was me playing tricks. But I was sleeping in my bed when it happened. Pretty strange.

As soon as I stepped into the den after my college classes the next day, the knocking began. It sounded like someone was striking the floorboards with a hammer. Except there's only a narrow crawl space under the floor of our den, and that's boarded up. I stared around the room, looking for an explanation while the pounding rattled the floorboard. The howling wind from the graveyard had died away to nothing—and there were no trees beside the house on that side. Blast. No explanation there.

Then the hammering noise stopped abruptly, and the room became unnaturally still. And I *felt* someone in there with me. Staring at me. Okay—that was too creepy for me. My backpack fell from my nerveless fingers as I backed out of the den. I bolted into the kitchen to ask my mother about the knocking noise. Loud as it had seemed in the den, Mom hadn't heard it in the kitchen. Double weird.

I had a lump in my throat the size of Texas when I crept down the hall to retrieve my backpack from the den. Was the invisible person still there? The room seemed empty. As I stepped inside, the TV turned on all by itself and started flipping wildly through the channels. The pounding of my heart was echoed by a throbbing in my temples as I dove forward, grabbed my backpack, and ran for the stairs. As soon as my sneakers hit the hallway, the TV turned off. Oh boy!

I went up to my room and called Fred. My hands were shaking so much I could hardly dial. "I think my den is haunted," I told him.

"Say again?" Fred said, bemused. I told him about the TV and about the knocking and about the invisible presence I felt in the den.

"Do you think Robah followed me home?" I asked nervously.

"Don't be silly," said Fred. But his voice had a note of uncertainty that I did not find comforting.

I did my homework in my room and didn't come down until Mom called me to supper. After washing up the dishes, I reluctantly joined my parents in the den, carrying a big bowl of popcorn. The fire was dancing merrily in the grate; the TV was burbling out a game show; Mom was piecing a quilt. Everything was normal. Relieved, I sat down on the loveseat with a book. And an invisible someone sat down next to me with a sigh of contentment.

I leapt so high that my bottom actually left the seat, and popcorn spilled everywhere. My parents gave me an odd look. "Be careful, Annie," Dad said from the recliner. Hastily, I handed the bowl of popcorn to my mom and crawled around on the floor, picking up popcorn and carefully avoiding the invisible person on the loveseat. Oddly, there was a person-size shape on the loveseat that was completely free of spilled popcorn. As I stared at it, a single kernel on top of the loveseat floated up into the air, as if it had been plucked up by an invisible hand,

and then disappeared in midair as if it had been popped into an invisible mouth.

Grabbing the last pieces of popcorn from the rug, I dumped them into the trash can and said, "I've got to finish my homework." Then I ran for the door. I heard Mom say, "Annie's acting very strange tonight," and Dad replied, "Kids!" Then I slammed shut the door of my room against invisible entities that ate popcorn. I called Fred. There was no way I was going to share my den with a ghost!

It turned out Fred was playing in a football game the following night, but he was free Friday evening. So I invited him to come to dinner with the family, and then we could do some ghost busting in the den while my parents went next door for their weekly game of bridge with the neighbors. Fred agreed.

I had trouble going to sleep that night, afraid the ghost would not confine its activities to the den. But aside from the sounds of late-night television coming from downstairs around 2:00 a.m.—softer this time so it wouldn't wake my parents—I didn't hear from the ghost again until the following afternoon. I was hovering in the hallway, holding a bag of potato chips and a soda, wondering if I should have my snack in the den with the ghost or eat it upstairs. Then the phone rang in the den. I went to answer it, dropping the open bag of chips and the can of soda onto the end table beside the loveseat.

The caller asked for my mom, so I ran to the kitchen to get her. As I left the room, I heard a loud crash. I hastened down the hall and stuck my head into the kitchen to tell Mom to pick up the phone extension by the refrigerator. Then, morbid with curiosity, I went back to the den to see what the invisible person had done this time. I found soda dripping down the wall of the den, and the crumpled can lying on the floor in a puddle of soda and soggy potato chips.

My heart pounded so hard that I felt as if I'd been running a marathon. "Okay, no soda or potato chips," I said aloud. "Next time I'll make popcorn."

There came an enthusiastic knocking from the floorboards under my feet. I *really* didn't like it when the ghost answered me! I backed out hastily to get paper towels and a mop to clean up the mess before Mom saw it. I didn't want to drag my parents into this ghostly business.

The room was silent and watchful as I cleaned the soda from the wall and picked up the soggy chips. When I hurried away, I heard the TV turn on all by itself. I made out the faint sounds of a game show as I climbed the stairs to my room. Only one more day, I thought grimly as I settled at my desk to do my homework. Then you're outta here, my ghostly friend!

Fred showed up promptly at 6:00 p.m. for dinner the next night. My parents were glad to see him. They liked Fred and approved of our relationship. When dinner was finished, my parents went next door to play their weekly game of bridge with the neighbors. They invited Fred and me, but we said we'd rather watch TV in the den.

As soon as they were gone, I dragged Fred down the hall. The moment he stepped foot in the den, the knocking began. Thud, thud, thud went the floorboards. Then the TV turned on and began roaming wildly from channel to channel. The lights flickered like strobes in a dance club.

"It's good to see you too, Robah," Fred shouted loudly. Immediately, the lights stopped flickering, the pounding stopped, and the TV settled itself onto another game show. Apparently, Robah was addicted to them.

Fred patted my hand reassuringly and then said aloud, "Thanks so much for coming to visit, Robah. But it's time to go home now."

Silence, save for the smarmy voice of the game-show host blaring from the TV.

"Come on out to the car, Robah," Fred said. He walked to the front door and shrugged into his coat, beckoning for me (and Robah) to follow him. So I did, putting on coat and scarf against the chilly autumn air. But the TV stayed on in the den.

We walked out to the car and got inside. Then we got back out, went back into the house, and stood in the doorway of the den. "Come on out to the car, Robah," Fred said again, very gently. "Time to go home."

He turned and walked back outside. Hesitantly, I followed him. This time, I heard the TV turn off, and a miniature whirlwind accompanied me to the car, tugging at my coat and scarf as I walked.

We drove to the graveyard in silence and parked in the same place we'd parked on Halloween. "Come on, Robah. We're almost home," said Fred to the empty backseat as we got out of the car. We held hands as we walked slowly down the hill to the tombstone where we'd had our alfresco picnic. A small breeze accompanied us down the slope, whistling through my hair and brushing gently against my cheek. When we reached the grave site, the wind grew fierce and strong, whirling around us and blowing dead leaves into the air. "Welcome home, Robah," I said, my voice steady despite my jangled nerves.

ROBAH

We waited for the breeze to die down before we went back to the car.

"Do you think it worked?" I asked Fred as we drove away.

"Only one way to find out," he said, and he took us back to my house. The den, when we entered, was blessedly silent and free of invisible presences. Our cans of soda and the big bag of potato chips we brought in with us remained untouched. And we had to turn on the TV when we wanted to see a program. It was a real relief.

"Guess Robah is gone," I said, reaching over to give Fred's hand a grateful squeeze.

"Looks like it," he said laconically. He brushed his fingers lightly against my cheek and added: "I think next year, we should go to a Halloween party. I've had enough of graveyards!"

"Me too," I nodded emphatically. "Me too!"

10

Busted!

It was the opportunity of a lifetime. That's what Abel said. Of course, that's what Abel always said when we started a new scam. But this time, it looked like he was right. Ghost busting was the way to go, Abel said. So that was the way we went.

We needed props to make us look convincing to potential customers, so we purchased secondhand robes of a standard variety to make us look ministerial. Jacob brought along his humongous old family Bible—the kind that took two hands to lift. And I supplied several handbells thoughtfully swiped from a set when the local church lost funding from the diocese and had to shut its doors. Armed with these, a gross of white candles, and other sacred objects of the "trade," we started our new career in ghost busting.

We'd lurk in the local bars downtown and spot older citizens of a more superstitious variety. Blatant eavesdropping on the tipsy produced a few leads, and a week after our initial investment in tools, we were at the house of a little old lady called Wanda, graciously accepting tea and biscuits and hearing all about the "banging in the attic" caused by her ghost. It kept her up at night. She was always nervous. Sometimes she heard footsteps overhead. This was, Abel assured Wanda, typical ghostly behavior, and it was a good thing she'd called us to come lay the spirit to rest.

In my opinion, the show we put on was worth every penny of the exorbitant fee we charged old lady Wanda out of her retirement fund. All three of us put on robes with miters, and Abel had given me a fancy crosier he had picked up at a costume store. We staked out the attic, making a huge circle of white candles, dripping "holy water" in every corner, on every window, and all over the door. Jacob stood in the center of the candle ring holding the huge Bible and looking suitably pious. I stood beside him holding one large handbell that struck a doleful note that reverberated through the boards of the dusty attic.

Since I was the only one who had studied Latin, it was my job to do the chanting. Abel "translated" the proceedings to Wanda as we proceeded with the ceremony. My favorite moment was when Jacob's face creased with horror and he staggered backward, holding up the Bible defensively toward the "phantom of the attic." I struck a valiant pose, rang the bell rapidly several times, and threw holy water over the "ghost."

"Hallelujah! Thank you, God!" Abel shouted from his observer's position. He pumped Wanda's hand enthusiastically. "Your ghost is gone, ma'am," he told her as we sagged dramatically with relief before straightening our shoulders and cleaning up the candle ring. Wanda told us we were fine boys and wrote us a large check from her pension. Better yet, she said she'd recommend us to all her friends. Our first endorsement!

"Any banging you hear up here now is just that large branch outside your windowpane," Abel told her, leading her to the window to show her the tall oak planted too close to the house. "Any footsteps are squirrels. Your ghost is gone!"

Wanda was as good as her word. Calls started pouring in. Mostly older folks with creaky houses and time on their hands. Oh, and we had one gig where we removed a "weeping baby" from a house shared by six pretty girls just out of college. Abel got a date out of that gig while Jacob and I got bitten by the raccoon we found living in their garage. We had to get rabies shots too, which really made us mad.

"Next time, *you're* carrying that heavy Bible, and I'm holding the hand of the pretty girl," Jacob told Abel sharply. I stood in the background looking noncommittal and refrained from mentioning the visit I'd paid the girls the next day to show them the wounds the "ghost" had given me. After that visit, my dating calendar was booked solid through February!

By this time, we had more than a hundred thousand dollars in the bank, and we were sitting pretty. Everyone was happy with our "services," and the cops hadn't heard a word about us—a state of affairs that was unusual for us at this stage of the game.

Our next gig was more than an hour outside the city, deep into the Smokies. It was an old Victorian monstrosity that must have been inspired by Asheville's Biltmore House, because it was constructed on a similar—if ever so slightly smaller—scale. We turned into a ragged, overgrown driveway at dusk, and our headlights picked out the looming atrocity with its saggy old porch, cracked windowpanes, peeling paint, and rotting roof.

"Are you sure we've got the right address?" Jacob asked nervously as I navigated the car over the ruts in the gravel driveway.

"This is the place," Abel said confidently from the backseat, where he sat by the huge Bible and box of candles. "They are going to pay us fifty thousand smackeroos to get rid of their ghost! That's half again what we've already earned so far from this gig. Makes you wish you'd really gone into the priesthood."

"Or not," I said sarcastically, thinking of my pleasantly full date book.

"See, here comes our host for the evening," Abel said, pointing to a hunched figure coming down the warped front steps.

"His name isn't Igor, is it?" asked Jacob, his eyes popping. I understood exactly what he meant. The hunched white-haired fellow looked as if he was the assistant of mad Dr. Jekyll or perhaps Dr. Frankenstein himself.

"We didn't prepare for vampires," I joked nervously as the old man walked up to the door of the car.

"Will you two shut up!" Abel growled from the backseat. He threw on his "best customer" smile and leapt out of the car to greet the old man. Now that the man was visible in the headlights, I saw that the "hunch" was made by a shotgun cradled on his right arm. The man had a long, flowing beard, a gnarled old face, and the meanest black eyes you've ever seen. Oh boy! This was a real mountain man! Forget about monsters. This old fellow looked hard enough to chase us all the way to China if we didn't deliver good service tonight.

"We've got a real mean ghost tonight, boys," Abel said as we decamped from the car and began gathering our paraphernalia from the backseat. "Mr. Hatfield here says it's a screaming head. Isn't that right, Amos?"

68

"S'right," said the tough little man, glaring at us and fingering his shotgun thoughtfully. "'Pears on top of the main staircase and comes rolling down in flames, screaming all the way."

"Sounds ghastly," Abel said cheerfully. "But we'll soon put it to rights. Come on, fellows, let's set up in the hallway."

The inside of the house was just as warped and creepy as the outside. Cobwebs festooned the walls and ceiling. The rooms were chilly and smelled of dust and mildew. Old sheets—once white but now gray with dust—covered all the furniture, making everything look ghostly. I swear there was even one portrait on the wall of the hallway that had eyes that moved!

"Can't rent out the place," the old man said defensively when he saw my disapproving stare at all the dust piled everywhere. "Folks are too plumb scared of the haint. N'point in keeping it clean if I can't rent it. You boys set it right fer me, and I'll keep you in business 'til it's time to retire!"

Out of the corner of my eye, I saw Abel rub his hands together in glee at the notion. Personally, I wasn't so sure. Of course, I didn't believe in ghosts myself. But if anyplace was haunted, this would be the place!

The staircase dominated the front foyer. It was wide enough to belong in Biltmore House and ran upward for twenty-five steps before disappearing into the upper story. It had a lovely oak railing, and the wall beside it featured portraits of stern-faced ancestral types. Near the bottom was a small landing, with two stairs angling off to the right to complete the bottom of an "L." A dreadful flowered runner in a faded red went up the center of the stairs, pooled on the landing, and then continued upward past the old folks in the portraits. Someone needed to do some serious redecorating of this house once we got it "busted."

We set up our candle circle just in front of the wooden archway that framed the staircase. I lit about fifty candles while Jacob sloshed "holy" water up and down the staircase and in the corners of the room, soaking his ceremonial black robes. Somehow, Abel wriggled out of carrying the heavy Bible—again—and stood by the front door with old man Amos as I straightened the miter on my head. I nodded once to Jacob, staggering already under the weight of the massive tome, stepped into the candle circle with my crosier and handbell, and began a long chant in completely nonsensical Latin. I'd had a lot of practice lately and sounded magnificent as I droned my way up and down the scale, punctuating the sentences with mournful tolls of the bell.

I was about three-quarters of the way through my chant and was preparing to gesture with my crosier toward the "phantom" of the house, when the laughter began. It was a supernatural sound that reached inside my body and triggered every nerve ending. It had a strange echo as if the voice were laughing inside a dark cavern. I exchanged alarmed glances with Jacob as the laugh grew louder, and I sneaked a look over my shoulder at Abel, who was several shades paler than he'd been a moment before.

Then, in a tone of doom, the voice spoke.

"I come!" it cried. "I come!"

"I go! I go!" Jacob gasped beside me, nearly on his knees under the weight of the heavy Bible.

"Don't talk nonsense, man. And stand up straight!" I snapped over the heavy beating of my heart. My skin felt clammy and cold, and sweat was trickling down my forehead and across my neck.

A green light sprang up at the top of the staircase. It hovered there for a moment and then started to spin itself into a face. It was a monster face—like a Gorgon. Wild hair streamed everywhere, and sharp teeth jutted up from the wide lips. The nose was twisted and broken, and the eyes were glowing with red flames. It opened its mouth and started to scream—a horrible loud shriek that made every hair on my body stand on end. Then it burst into flames and rolled straight down the staircase toward us, making the turn at the end with the grace born of long experience. It headed right toward the candle ring!

I dropped the handbell and leapt backward, holding the crosier in front of me for protection. Unfortunately, my robes went right through the candle flames and caught fire. I staggered backward toward the door, slapping at the flames, unable to tear my horrified gaze from the approaching phantom. Its green head blazed with phantom red flames, and its scream made me want to wriggle right out of my crawling skin.

Jacob was facedown in the center of the candle ring, the Bible held over his head when the phantom reached him. To my horror, I saw him rise up—Bible and all—as if he were carried on a massive wind. Then he was tossed right past me through one of the wide windows framing the door. Jacob gave a shout of terror as glass shattered everywhere. Abel and I were littered with the shards, and tiny red cuts covered my face and hands.

I noticed peripherally that Amos seemed to have disappeared from the hallway, but that was all I had time to note before the head came for me. Abel was struggling desperately with the latch on the front door as the phantom wind wrapped around

Busted!

me with the force of a giant's fist. I was sent flying upward right through the ceiling. Plaster and boards and jagged ends of wood cascaded around me. I would have been knocked out if I hadn't had the miter on my head. I was lifted so high that my head hit the ceiling of the third story before the phantom fist dropped me onto the second-story floor. Somehow, I rolled onto my feet and dove straight for the front window. Thankfully, my subconscious had remembered there was a front porch. I fell only a few feet before I hit the rotting roof of the porch and crashed through it, down onto the glass-strewn boards below.

Inside the house I heard Abel screaming. The front door burst open beside me, and Abel staggered backward through it, covered in glowing green flames. The bodiless head was laughing again, and it was three times the size it had been when it first appeared. I leapt to my feet, grabbed Abel by the flaming arm—a heroic act on my part—and hustled him off the porch into the yard. Jacob was in the car already, frantically trying to turn around in the narrow driveway. We approached the car at a run. I wrenched open the door and flung Abel and myself into the backseat.

Fortunately for all, the green flames covering Abel extinguished as soon as we entered the vehicle. Jacob gunned the motor, and we raced out of the driveway and down the hill with such speed that the wheels of the car sometimes left the ground on the tighter curves. None of us spoke. We were shaking with reaction, and all of us were bleeding from the cuts we'd received when the window broke. Plus I had a huge bump on my head where it had crashed through the ceiling.

Jacob didn't slow the car until we reached the outskirts of Asheville. "I don't know about you two, but my ghost-busting days are over," he announced as we entered the city. Abel and I heartily concurred.

I found out later that Abel had gotten tipsy when he went out with the pretty girl from the crying-baby house and had let it slip that a raccoon—not a ghost—had inflicted those wounds on Jacob and me. Since her family ran an illegal moonshine business on the side, she didn't want to go to the police about our little scam. So she asked her Uncle Amos to introduce us to a real ghost to pay us back for our little deception. So in the end, we were the ones who got busted!

11

The Rescue

WILMINGTON

That stormy night in the winter of 1897 was undoubtedly the strangest and most terrifying evening I've ever spent on the river. At the time, I was captain of a steamer and ran a ferry service out of Wilmington. On the night in question, we were bound for Southport. Heavy sleet was thundering down on the ship, it was pitch dark, and ice was floating on the river. It made for a difficult run. Frankly, I was steering more by instinct and the memory of hundreds of previous trips, rather than by sight.

Our only passenger stayed up top in the pilothouse with me, keeping warm and dry and entertaining me with sea stories. He was an elderly man from Scotland, and I quite liked him in spite of his tendency to ramble. There was a twinkle in his eyes that bespoke a good heart.

As we made slow progress toward Southport, he related a story about one of his ancestors who had come to America just before the Revolutionary War. Having distinguished himself at the Battle of Culloden in the Highlands, this illustrious ancestor was invited to join the Scottish settlement in Cape Fear by no less a personage than colonial governor Gabriel Johnson. The

Highland Scot took to his new home with enthusiasm, and when the American Revolution came, he sided with the rebels.

The Highlander's activities did not go unnoticed by the British troops stationed at Wilmington. He was captured along with two other Whigs and imprisoned in the hull of a prison ship in the harbor to await his death. At the appointed hour, the three manacled men were placed onto an old barge and poled out to a place near the ruins of Governor Tryon's palace. They stood trial there and were sentenced to death. The two Whigs were led out first, bound to a large tree, and then shot to death by a firing squad. The Highlander was then brought forth and released from his shackles, preparatory to binding him to the same tree where the Whigs had just perished. For a single moment, the Highlander was free and unbound. And in that moment, he sprang forth, knocking his guards aside and running away into the forest. The British soldiers followed immediately, but the Highlander was too quick for them. He evaded recapture and eventually made his way home safely, just as the war ended and the British left the South for good. "He was lucky," I said to fill the pause that followed. Another lash of sleet hit the window of the pilothouse. I peered fruitlessly into the darkness ahead, hoping I was still on course.

"Very lucky," the passenger said. "He lived out the full length of his days and died in 1800. The other Whigs weren't so lucky." He paused for a moment and glanced sideways at me as if to gauge my reaction to his next remark. Then he said, "On stormy nights, the ghosts of the manacled Scotsmen are sometimes seen floating on a barge in the port near Brunswick. Perhaps they are reliving their final moments, hoping for a better ending?"

A huge gust of wind slammed against the pilothouse, rattling the windows and driving sleet sharply against the roof. I shuddered a bit, remembering the whispers I'd heard up and down the river about the ghostly barge seen floating in the harbor. At least now I knew the story behind the spirits.

The storm was growing worse, and conversation lagged as my attention was needed for the tricky piloting. I was afraid we would founder as the storm worsened, becoming in ferocity as strong as a hurricane. My crew were taking soundings constantly, trying to keep us in the channel. Then one of the deckhands burst into the pilothouse, shouting that we had lost the channel and were drifting toward some jetties. The next moment, the steamer rattled from stem to stern, caught fast on an underwater jetty. I raced out into the storm, slipping and sliding on the sleet-covered deck. A quick assessment told me we were locked down until the turn of the tide, but otherwise the steamer was unharmed.

Since we had an hour or so before the turn of the tide, I ordered the crew belowdecks to stay warm and dry in the furnace room, leaving only the first mate on duty outside. Then I returned to the pilothouse to keep my solo passenger company while we waited. About fifteen minutes after the accident, Jorgenson, the mate working the decks, came sliding into the pilothouse, white as a sheet, ice crystals shimmering on the ends of his hair.

"Sir! I saw . . . I saw . . ." Jorgenson's face contorted, and he stopped abruptly, shaking from head to toe. In his agitation, he dropped the lantern he was holding onto the floor.

"Calm down, man," I barked. "What did you see?"

Jorgenson rubbed his face with shaking hands. "There was a man," he began again. "I saw a bearded man in rough, tattered clothes appear suddenly by the rail, clutching at it as if it were a lifeline, and his face was . . ." Jorgenson shuddered and changed course in mid-sentence. "Well, let's just say he was terrified. He pointed out into the storm with his left hand. I ran over to help him, but when I grabbed at his arm to help him aboard, he . . . vanished!"

The passenger and I both exclaimed in disbelief.

"You've had too much to drink," I said, shaking my head. But Jorgenson insisted it was true. So I swept the lantern from where it lay on the floor, shrugged into my wet-weather gear, and made a search of the deck. The Scottish passenger helped me search, but Jorgenson refused to leave the refuge of the pilothouse. Of course, we found nothing but icy decks, pouring sleet, and howling rain.

Jorgenson still looked a little green when we got back to the pilothouse. I poured all of us a drink while I related the results of our search. The mate insisted that he had seen a phantom at the rail.

"The lantern light struck him full in the face," Jorgenson said. "I couldn't have been mistaken."

Agreeing to disagree, we waited another forty-five minutes for the turning tide and the steady rotation of the propellers to shift us off the underwater jetty. Then we were back in the channel and on our way down the stormy river, rolling in the heavy waves but moving steadily forward.

As I navigated cautiously through the maelstrom, a storm-tossed gull slammed suddenly into the window of the pilothouse, smashing the glass and landing at the feet of our Scottish passenger.

"A bad omen," he gasped, staring down at the panting, bleeding gull lying at his feet. Icy air filled the pilothouse, and I stared from the passenger's white face to Jorgenson's shaking hands.

"'Tis a ghostly night, surely. But not all omens are bad," I said finally, to lighten the mood. "Put the poor creature somewhere warm until it recovers. And Jorgenson, why don't you set up an extra watch, just in case any more ghosts decide to appear for us tonight! If the crew are busy, they won't be so likely to panic if they see a phantom."

My jocular tone reassured the passenger and the mate. The passenger blocked up the broken pane as best he could while Jorgenson arranged for a special watch to give the nervous crew something useful to do.

As the crew moved briskly about the deck, I steered us carefully through the huge storm waves and falling ice. The wind shook the pilothouse again and again as our solo passenger mildly discussed other terrible storms he'd seen over the years. Various crew members, back on duty now that we were moving, came in and out of the pilothouse as they went about their allotted tasks, and everything seemed normal.

Then we heard a sharp human scream coming from the farther shore. It pierced even the fierce blowing of the wind and the sharp staccato of sleet on the roof. I jumped, and my hands started shaking on the wheel.

"By all that is holy! What was that?" gasped the passenger. The crew crowded into the pilothouse, exclaiming in confusion. The fear in the air was palpable now. To calm things down, I ordered a full stop. The engines cut out, and suddenly the sound of the storm was much louder. The ship started to roll as it settled into the trough of a large wave. And then, over the roar of the storm, the scream came again.

At that moment I realized where we were. The scream was coming from the direction of the old anchorage where the colonial prison ship once held three Highland Whigs waiting for death. Pulse pounding madly in my throat and wrists, I ordered all the crew to take special watches around the deck to see if we could spot the source of the scream. Sleet pummeled us as we strained our eyes in the wave-tossed darkness. Over the howling wind, the scream came a third time. And then we saw it.

Out in the darkness where the old ship had anchored, a dark object became visible through great sheets of rain and sleet. It glowed with a phosphorescent light, and in that light I saw an ancient rowing barge, slimy with seaweed and gnarled with barnacles. It looked as if it hadn't been used in a hundred years or more. It was a ghastly vision, and I was transfixed at the sight. My legs were shaking so badly that I could barely stand, but I kept my voice calm as I ordered the men to be ready to heave a line to the stricken vessel. They prepared to obey, straining eyes forward toward the ancient barge. By now we could make out two huge, gaunt figures in tattered Highland kilts standing on the barge. There were heavy chains around their legs and arms, and their wrists and ankles were raw and bleeding from the rubbing shackles. When they saw our steamer, both men reached forward as far as the chains would allow, beckoning us to their aid. I swallowed heavily, cleared my throat, and again ordered the mate to throw them a line.

Jorgenson, hands trembling visibly from the gruesome sight, heaved the line over the side. At that moment the barge and ship were both slammed by a huge storm wave. Everyone shouted and grabbed for a solid surface as water poured everywhere. The steamer rocked heavily and remained upright. But the barge was swallowed up by the wave, and the line floated unclaimed in the water. We searched the dark, stormy waves with our lanterns, but the ghastly barge with its tattered prisoners had vanished as surely as Jorgenson's phantom.

Finally, I ordered the engines started, and we moved downriver in the direction of the floating barge, all hands keeping watch for the vanished vessel. Maybe the men we'd seen had been the Highland phantoms from our passenger's story, or maybe they weren't. I wasn't taking any chances, though. If injured or capsized men were out there, we would find them and bring them aboard.

After ten minutes of searching, one of the watchers gave a mighty shout. A wreck had been sighted. We changed course quickly to avoid crashing into the ship, which had gone bottom up. Through the howling wind and raging sleet, two figures could be discerned clinging to the overturned hull. We immediately came to the rescue, and soon both men had been brought aboard ship.

As the light of the lantern fell on the face of the first, Jorgenson gasped and grabbed hold of the wall in the pilothouse to steady himself. It was the bearded "phantom" who had appeared to him at the rail of the steamer earlier that evening! Furthermore, Jorgenson had seen the man pointing along the river in the direction where we'd found the wreck, which—coincidentally—was the same direction the Highlanders on the barge had been drifting when they beckoned for us to follow them.

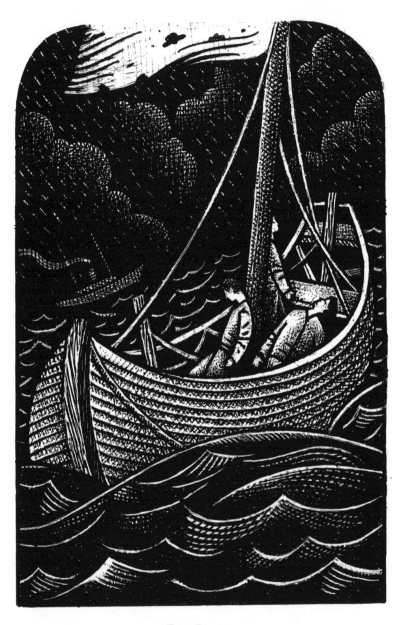

THE RESCUE

The two men were all that remained of the seven-person crew of their ship. The other five crew members had been swept overboard during the storm and drowned. The two survivors had clung to the hull of the ship for hours, calling out over the storm as best they could while they gradually lost strength and their hope of rescue grew dim.

I piloted the steamer with its three passengers safely into Southport that night and waited out the storm before returning to Wilmington, which gave me plenty of time to mull over the events of that frightening evening. If we hadn't heard the phantom screaming and seen the glowing Highland barge, we would not have been watching the river for survivors and would have crashed right into the wrecked ship. And what of the man seen by Jorgenson clutching desperately to the rail of the steamer? Was it possible that the spirit of a man wrecked miles away could really span the distance between our ships to summon us to his rescue? It remains a mystery to this day.

12

Plucked

MURPHY

Hard times fell on the Mortimer family after the war. Penury forced them out of their home, and they moved into an old cabin at the outskirts of town to scratch what living they could from the land. The missus was a bitter woman by the time her man up and died, leaving her with two little boys to feed. She'd come from a wealthy family, but they'd thrown her out when she married, and they wouldn't take her back after her man passed.

The Mortimer boys were raised hard. Every attitude of their bitter, selfish, money-loving mother was embraced by them to the full. They looked down on their neighbors and picked fights with all the local children. When the oldest chap was twelve, they built a still up in the holler and started running moonshine across the state line to earn a little cash. When they couldn't sell shine, they went to the local school to cheat their school chums out of some cash. The brothers would set up card games, bully the other boys into playing, and then fleece their classmates of every penny. When the schoolboys protested, the eldest Mortimer made a great show of cleaning his gun while the younger Mortimer started sharpening his knife with a flint.

The schoolboys got the hint and took off quick, leaving their money behind.

Drinking, hunting, quarreling, and swindling became a way of life for the Mortimer boys. So it shouldn't have come as a surprise when the missus got her finger shot off one day when she interfered in a quarrel between her two lads. They were having a shouting match over $4 that the younger Mortimer had borrowed from the elder and couldn't pay back. The shouting got so loud that it gave the missus a headache. So she marched out to the gate to give both her lads a licking. Unfortunately for her, that was the moment the elder Mortimer boy pulled out his gun. Unfortunately for him, the bullet meant to scare his brother into coughing up the cash not only took off his mama's middle finger but also entered the forehead of his baby brother, killing him instantly. But the judge was real understanding about it. After all, the younger Mortimer brother had pulled a knife on his brother. So the killing was ruled as self-defense.

"Served him right," the elder Mortimer muttered defensively to his mama, standing at the graveside of his younger brother. "He shouldn't a' borrowed the money if'n he couldn't pay it back."

What could the missus say to that? He was quoting the very words she'd used herself so many times, railing against the foolishness of her neighbors.

The elder Mortimer didn't want to admit that he missed his brother. Now there was no one to participate in his money-making schemes, no one to help with the still. Everyone in town was avoiding him, and the judge had told him straight out that if the elder Mortimer appeared in his courtroom again, he'd get twenty years in the slammer.

The night after the burial, the elder Mortimer boy had a strange dream. In his dream his younger brother came to him, white-faced and dead, with a red bullet hole in his forehead. He floated bonelessly up to the bed where the elder Mortimer lay, reached down with icy-cold fingers, and yanked a single strand from his brother's bushy red hair. It hurt like the dickens. The elder Mortimer let out a yell and woke himself up. His scalp was stinging where the ghost had touched it. When he rubbed it, a clump of hair fell out, plucked from his head by the roots.

"Maaa!" the elder Mortimer wailed in panic, rubbing at the bald spot on his head.

The missus came running, shocked to see her tough son wide-eyed as a frightened baby. She examined the small bald spot and firmly told him a mouse must have gotten into his bed and nibbled off his hair. The elder brother, shaking with cold, tried to believe her. But he couldn't figure out how a mouse could pluck hairs out by the roots.

The next night, almost as soon as he closed his eyes, the elder Mortimer boy saw his younger brother floating through the open window of the cabin. The dead boy's face was a hollow mask under the grotesque red hole in his forehead. His cheeks had withered overnight, collapsing inward like the cheeks of an ancient man, and his blue eyes were wide open and staring sightlessly at nothing. The elder Mortimer lay paralyzed with fright as the corpse drifted nearer, stretching out its hand toward his head. Cold fingers ran through his scalp and then yanked hard.

The elder Mortimer woke with a scream and sat up, huge chunks of hair scattering all over the bed and onto the floor— plucked out by the roots. The missus came running when she heard him, and she couldn't explain away the huge bald patch covering the right half of her boy's head, from his forehead all the way down to his neck.

"I'm being hainted," the elder boy wailed, wringing his hands like a tiny child. "Make it stop, Mama! Make it stop!"

"I'll get a preacher-man to come pray over the cabin," the missus said. "That'll frighten away any haints, don't you worry."

The elder Mortimer brother was comforted by this plan, but he still sat up the rest of the night feeding the fire to keep the cabin nice and bright. At dawn he went up to the holler and spent the day making moonshine while his mama called the preacher-man out to exorcise the haint. But he was tired out after his long, sleepless night. He lay down by the still to get some rest.

And dreamed of his younger brother. The dead boy's skin was rotting away from his face and hands, revealing bone underneath his eyes and allowing his sagging nose to collapse inward. The red bullet hole gaped in his forehead, and his dead head lolled against his shoulder. His white hands, bones poking through his fingertips, stretched out toward his brother's hair and pulled . . .

The elder Mortimer boy screamed himself awake, hair showering all around him, spilling over the boards of the still and across the dirt floor. He clutched at his head, which was plucked bald. With a long, wordless wail, he ran down the hill and burst into the cabin, where the preacher-man was standing with his holy book and a goblet of holy water. The boy fell to his knees in front of the preacher-man.

"Make it stop! Make it stop!" he sobbed, his bald head pressed against the man's shiny black shoes.

PLUCKED

Plucked

Behind him, the door was caught by a huge blast of frigid air. The wind slammed the door so hard that it splintered and sagged on its hinges. Filling the doorway was a rotting corpse, maggots writhing in and out of its eye sockets, bones gaping through withered gray skin, head lolling against bare shoulder bones. Its forehead was dominated by a huge, bloodstained bullet hole. It staggered forward on bony legs, its withered hands reaching toward the elder Mortimer boy.

The preacher screamed. The missus screamed.

The skeleton's fingers closed on the scraggly beard growing from the boy's chin . . . and yanked.

The elder Mortimer boy convulsed once against the preacher's shiny black shoes. Then he rolled onto his back, mouth agape, eyes staring sightlessly up at the holy book and goblet still held in the minister's hands. Every single hair had been plucked from his body—arms, legs, face, hands, and torso. Small red hairs were slowly raining down onto the dirt floor of the cabin, covering every surface and sprinkling the heads of the preacher-man and the missus. A few hairs landed in the holy goblet.

The missus screamed and ran. She ran out of the house, out of the yard, out of the town, and kept running. She was never seen again. The preacher, made of sterner material, wiped the hair off his holy book, said a prayer over the plucked corpse of the elder Mortimer boy, and carried him back to the churchyard to be buried.

After the deaths of the two Mortimer brothers, no one would go near the haunted cabin just outside town. In a few seasons it rotted away until only a few boards and a broken-down chimney were left to show where it once stood.

89

13

The Headless Haunt

MADISON

The evening was windy and cold. It was a bad night to be out walking, but the old man and his wife kept pushing their way through the thick mud on the road, trying to reach their son's house. Darkness had fallen swiftly, and threatening clouds hovered overhead.

"Mother, I reckon my feet are nigh on frozen," the old man said after a while. "And I'm hungry enough to eat a horse."

"Well, Father, I think we should find a place to stay the night," his wife replied, hugging her shawl tightly around her. "I reckon Junior won't mind if we don't arrive till morning."

Heartened by this decision, the old couple kept watch for a place to spend the night. Soon they saw a house through the thick trees that lined the muddy road. As they approached, they saw that it was quite a grand house, with smoke rising from the chimney and firelight flickering in many windows.

"Father, I reckon the folks who live here are rich," the old woman said to her husband. "We'd best go around to the back door."

"Whatever you think best," said the old man, who didn't care which door they used, as long as they got in out of the cold.

They went around to the back porch and knocked on the door. A man's voice called, "Come in." So in they went.

They found themselves in a large kitchen with a fire in the hearth and skillets waiting as if someone was about to prepare supper. But there was no one in the room. They looked around, but they didn't see the man who bade them enter. The old woman saw a rabbit boiling in a covered pot, and she smelled beans baking. On the wide wooden table were meat and flour and lard.

"Somebody's cooking dinner," the old woman told her husband, who was warming his hands over the fire. "I wonder where they be?"

"Seems a bit strange, them running off just after they told us to come in," said the old man. "But meanwhile, Mother, take off your wet shoes and stockings and get yourself warmed up. I'll run out and fill up those buckets at the springhouse we passed so we can have some coffee. Maybe our host will make himself known while I'm outside."

"I'll get the brown beans and that molly cottontail and that cornbread ready for our dinner in three shakes of a lamb's tail," the old woman said with relish as she took off her wet shoes and stockings.

The old man went out with a bucket, and the old woman sat down by the fire to toast her feet. She was just thinking about getting up and mixing up some cornbread when right through the shut door came a man with no head. The old woman gasped in fear and astonishment. The man was wearing britches, a vest, shirt, coat, and shoes. He even wore a fancy collar. But rising above it was a bloody stump where his head should have been.

"What in the name of the Lord do you want?" the old woman gasped.

And the man started to talk to her without any mouth. The words seemed to form themselves in the old woman's head as he told her how he came to be this way.

"I am in misery, madam," the man said. "I was killed by a robber who was after my money. He removed my head with a cutlass and then took me to the cellar and buried my head on one side and my body on the other. Then this villain and his companions dug all around my cellar, but fortunately they did not find my treasure. Alas, they went away and left me in two pieces, doomed to haunt this house until someone should restore my head and bury me in one grave."

The old woman was moved by the ghost's story. "How is it no one has ever restored you?" she asked.

"There have been others, madam, who have entered this house. But as none addressed me in the name of the Lord, I was unable to speak to them."

At that moment the door swung open, passing right through the body of the ghost. The old man hurried in with his bucket full of water, stamping his feet to get the mud off.

"Mother, it's plumb cold out there," he said, setting the bucket on the shelf. He turned back toward the door, intending to shut it, and saw the ghost. The old man gasped and backed away, his horrified gaze on the bloody stump where the ghost's head should be.

"It's all right, Father," the old woman said hastily, closing the door against the cold. "Sir, please tell my husband your tale, in the name of the Lord."

So the ghost told the old man his story. When the ghost finished, he asked the old couple to go to the cellar and find his head so he could be buried in one grave.

"If, in your kindness, you restore me, I will show you where my treasure is buried," the headless haunt concluded.

The old man looked at his wife, who nodded. "We will surely help you," he told the ghost. "Just let me get a torch and a shovel."

"You will not need a torch," said the ghost. With great dignity, he walked to the fire and stuck his finger in it. The finger blazed up as bright as any torch. He pointed to the place where the shovels were kept and then led the old couple down into the dark cellar by the light of his finger.

"There. That is where my head is buried," said the ghost, pointing toward the north end of the cellar, "and there is where my body is buried," he finished, pointing toward a hole in the south corner. "But dig here first, and you will find my barrels of silver and gold."

The headless haunt lit up a section of the floor, and the old couple started to dig. They dug until the old woman was almost worn out. They were deep under the cellar floor. Then the old man's shovel made a hollow thump as he pushed it into the soil, and they soon uncovered several barrels filled with gold and silver. The old woman sat on her heels, running her fingers through the beautiful coins, lit by the blazing finger of the ghost. With tears in her eyes, she said, "Oh, thank you, sir. Thank you. And now, we must restore your head to you."

Her husband, who was staring speechlessly at the gold and silver, came out of his trance and said, "That we must,

Mother. Good sir, if you will show us again where your head is buried?"

The old man helped his wife out of the pit and they followed the ghost to the corner where his head was buried. A few turns of the shovel produced the head, and the husband lifted it with the shovel and offered it to the ghost. The haunt reached over with dignity, took his head in his hands, and put it on his neck. Then he lit several candles with his burning finger so the old couple would have light to remove the gold and silver from the pit they had dug. He blew out his finger and, still keeping a firm grip on his head, walked over to the south corner and sank through the floor into the place where his body was buried. Just before his head sank into the ground, he said, "Thank you, good sir and kind madam."

As soon as the last bit of the ghost disappeared, the ground shook and the house trembled above their heads. Then a voice came from under the ground: "You have restored me! I am now buried together, head and corpse. Because of your kindness, I give you my lands, my house, and my money. May you be as rich as I was, and come to a more honorable end."

The old man and his wife stared at one another in shock for a moment. Then the old woman smiled and picked up one of the candles the headless haunt had lit for them.

"Come, Father," she said. "We have the rest of our lives to count this gold. But that cottontail will be boiled over if we wait much longer to eat supper."

The old man took the other candle and helped his wife up the stairs. They were covered with dirt from their digging, so they washed themselves clean with lye soap. Then the old woman mixed up a batch of cornbread and the old man made

The Headless Haunt

some coffee with the water from the springhouse and they had a wonderful supper of cottontail and cornbread and brown beans and hot coffee.

And the old man and the old woman lived in the grand house for the rest of their days, with money to spare for food and clothing. When they died at last of old age, they left a large inheritance for their grandchildren. And no one ever saw the headless haunt again.

14

Haunted Gun

CATALOOCHEE

We sat looking at the casket as the preacher spoke a few words to comfort the bereaved. My cousin Ethel wept softly, clinging to her young 'uns, who were still stunned by the loss of their father. A fever took Jimmy way too early, and the whole community mourned with the family.

My wife, Martha, gave Ethel a hug and kiss once the burial was over, and I patted her shoulder awkwardly.

"You'll stay for supper?" Ethel asked us. "Jimmy had something he wanted me to give to you."

A gift? That surprised me, but I should have expected it. Jimmy and I were close as kin. We grew up together in the Cataloochee Valley, and Jimmy first met Ethel at my house when she came to visit my folks. I'd been best man at their wedding.

"A neighbor's daughter is watching our boys, so we can stay as long as you want," Martha said.

Ethel's small house was overflowing with family and neighbors. My wife went straight to the kitchen to help set out the food while a couple of us did chores to help the new widow.

After dinner, Ethel led me outside to Jimmy's "office." It was just a fixed-up corner in the old woodshed, but Jimmy and I'd spent many a happy hour there drinking and relaxing whenever the house got too loud. I had to blink hard to keep from crying when Ethel walked me back there.

Ethel went to the fancy carved desk Jimmy had made with his own hands and pulled a pistol out of the drawer. That did me in completely. I sat down and wept worse than the young 'uns. Jimmy was right proud of that pistol. He'd bought it about a month ago from a tourist who came to the valley to fish and never got to use it. Jimmy took sick that same evening and the gun had set out in the woodshed office ever since.

"Your boy should have that pistol," I told Ethel, wiping my eyes.

"No," she said at once. "Jimmy wanted you to have something of his. When the boy asked for his Pa's rifle, Jimmy said to give you this to remember him by."

What could I say? It was too much, but I could tell from my cousin's face that protesting would offend her. I accepted the pistol.

Ethel nodded as if she could read my thoughts. "There's plenty of bears and wild panthers out there. Carrying a pistol is a good idea when you are walking outside after dark," she said.

"Yes ma'am. It will come in handy this evening when I escort my missus home," I said, rising from the chair. "Something I need to do right now, as it happens. It's near dark and we've got a few miles to cover."

Martha and I said goodbye to Ethel and walked out to the road. I showed my wife the pistol Jimmy gave me as we walked toward our home on the far side of the valley. Then I put it into my pocket and took her hand like we were still courting. It wasn't often I got to step out with my bride without our young 'uns in tow. We'd been wed for many years, but I still knew how to make her giggle and blush.

We were about a mile from our place when a strange man appeared, walking silently next to my wife in the twilight. That was odd. Neither of us heard him approach. He was just suddenly there. I called a greeting, but he didn't answer. I gripped the pistol in my pocket, not sure if the fellow was shy or if he was a troublemaker. Folks often joined up with a group for safety's sake, especially if they were walking alone after dark. But generally, a fellow would introduce himself and talk to the people he was accompanying. This silent stranger raised goosebumps on my arms and legs. Something wasn't quite right. However, he wasn't threatening us, and having a third person with us helped keep the bears and panthers at bay. I'd just keep my eye on him.

I was so busy minding my thoughts that I stumbled over a rock in the road. The stranger stumbled at the same moment. That was bizarre. Martha and I exchanged confused glances. Was the stranger deliberately mimicking me, or was it just a coincidence? I shrugged, and so did the stranger. I stopped. So did the stranger. When I continued, the stranger did too. Martha stared back and forth between us, perplexed by the strangeness of the man's behavior.

To confirm my suspicions, I pointed toward the bend in the road and said: "We're nearly at our turnoff." The stranger pointed at the same moment and his mouth moved, but no words came out.

"Why is he acting so strange?" Martha whispered, but I didn't have an answer.

"Just keep going," I murmured. "If he follows us into the yard, I'll make him leave."

We quickened our pace and turned off at the bend in the road. The stranger followed us. Martha's lips tightened, and I patted the pocket containing the pistol to reassure her. Then I hurried my wife into the house and turned to confront the stranger, pistol in hand. He was gone. I searched the yard and all the outbuildings, but the stranger had vanished.

The presence of a stranger in the vicinity made me nervous, so I walked the neighbor's daughter home and warned her folks about the stranger before I went to check on the livestock. Then I locked up the house good and tight and put the pistol next to the bed before we went to sleep.

It was almost midnight when a breeze blew the covers off me and Martha, startling us awake.

"What in tarnation?" I shouted, clutching for the bedclothes, which were tangled at the foot of the bed.

The stranger walked into our bedroom and marched to the foot of the bed. Martha screamed and I jumped out of bed, waving my pistol. Instantly, the stranger vanished.

"The boys," Martha cried. She ran to check on the young 'uns. I was right on her heels. The boys were sleeping peacefully in the loft. The stranger was nowhere to be seen.

I lit the lamp and we checked the door. The bolts were still engaged and there was no sign of a forced entry.

"Did he come through a window?" she asked.

"See for yourself," I said, gesturing to the wooden shutters I'd pulled tight before bed. Martha tested each one, but they were still locked. Her face was pale when she looked me in the eye.

"Is it a ha'nt?" she asked.

"I think so," I replied. "I don't know what else it could be."

HAUNTED GUN

We went back to bed, both of us shaking with nerves. I didn't think I would fall asleep, but I must have, because I was startled awake when the bedroom door opened a second time and a breeze shook the room. As before, the stranger walked right up to our bed.

I knew my ha'nt stories. You were supposed to talk to the ghost to find out why it was ha'nting you. I sat bolt upright and grabbed the pistol. Pointing it at the spirit, I said: "Who are you and what do you want?"

The stranger didn't reply. He just faded away, as before.

Martha was watching this second encounter with wide eyes. She said, "I think the ha'nt is tied to that gun. It showed up right after we left Ethel's place and now it's coming into the bedroom to look for the pistol."

"Why would Ethel give us a ha'nted gun?" I asked, lighting the lamp so we could study the pistol. There were no scratch marks or initials or anything that would give us a clue to its previous ownership.

"She probably didn't know about the ghost. Didn't you say that Jimmy never used it?" Martha replied.

"That's right," I said. "He got sick before he could try it out. And he kept it in his woodshed office, so the spirit would have stayed back there. No wonder Jimmy got such a good price for the pistol. That tourist was trying to get rid of the ha'nt."

"You'd best put that pistol in *our* woodshed for the night or we won't get any sleep," said Martha firmly. "And you are selling the gun in the morning. No arguments."

The ghost fell into step beside me as soon as I exited the house, and it accompanied me to the woodshed.

"Sorry, stranger. No fancy office here," I said, putting the gun in a notch under the roof. "We will find you a new home in the morning."

The ghost didn't say a word. It just strode into the woodshed and the door slammed shut in a supernatural gust of wind.

I was going to Tennessee in the morning to take care of some family business. I'd sell the pistol when I got there. I hoped Jimmy wouldn't mind me selling his memorial gift. If he did, his ha'nt just might pay us a visit. Still, better Jimmy than an unknown ghost, I decided, leaving the spirit and its gun in the woodshed and heading back to bed.

15

The Cavern of Skulls

NANTAHALA NATIONAL FOREST

There was once a farmer who lived in these here hills who built his settler cabin near a cave. He didn't know the cave was there, until the day the farmer found his old hound dog chewing on a human bone. The farmer took the bone from him and studied it. It looked real old and brittle.

"Where'd you get this old bone?" the farmer asked the dog. The hound sniffed the bone and then set off at a run, eager to find a replacement. The farmer followed his dog through the forest until the dog disappeared behind some shrubbery. When the farmer thrust it aside, he felt a rush of cool air and saw the large mouth of a cave.

When the farmer cautiously followed his hound dog into the cave, he stumbled over a half-buried skull. The farmer gave a shriek of terror, and then laughed at his own foolishness. The person that skull belonged to was long dead. He explored the cavern as far as the light from the entrance would allow, promising himself that he'd come back later with a lantern. He noticed there were a great many skulls piled up inside and decided the cave must have been a burial ground many years before.

Now the polite and respectful thing would have been to leave the old bones where they'd been laid to rest. But the farmer wasn't polite nor respectful when it came to money. He saw the skulls as an opportunity to save some cash. You see, the last time he and his missus went to town, a traveling salesman had been selling a special fertilizer that he claimed would make vegetables grow twice as big. The missus's eyes got real big when he showed her a squash the size of her butter churn. She wanted her husband to buy some of that fertilizer, but the cost was sky high and the farmer said no. The missus had been plaguing the daylights out of him ever since. The farmer figured he could take these old bones and grind them up for fertilizer so his missus would stop her nagging.

"The owners won't mind a bit," he told his hound dog, who was chewing on an arm bone. "They are long-gone. And the missus will be right grateful."

So the farmer got some sacks and filled them up with skulls. Then he hauled them back to his farm in a cart and tumbled them any old how into his shed. Just then, his missus came to the door of the cabin and shouted out that dinner was cooked, so the farmer shut the shed door and went to eat his supper.

"What you got in all those sacks?" asked the missus as she ladled soup into his bowl.

"I got some of that fertilizer you've been hankering for," the farmer said.

The missus squealed with happiness and gave him a smooch that nearly knocked his socks off. What with one thing and another, the farmer didn't get around to grinding down the skulls that evening.

It was as dark and still as any night you'd ever seen in these mountains when the farmer snuggled down in bed sleep with his missus, who was happier than a young 'un about her fertilizer. He was sleeping sound when a roar like the coming of a big cyclone woke him. The farmer raced to the window, a-fearing the house was going to be swept away. "Margie, get up right now," he shouted. "We gotta get down into the root cellar."

But when the farmer looked outside, the night was calm and still. There were no clouds in the sky. No wind rustling in the trees. He didn't even hear the chirping of the crickets or the rustling of night critters in the bushes. The forest was so quiet it gave him goose bumps. The silence weighed on the farmer as if he were covered in a thick wool blanket. It was hard to breathe in the dead air.

The farmer's hands were shaking when he tried to rouse his missus. He needed the sound of her voice to drive away the threatening silence. But his missus wouldn't wake. It was like she was under some kind of sleeping spell.

The farmer hollered for his hound dog to come, but his voice sounded thin and stretched. It echoed slightly, like he was talking into a tin cup. The sound was strangled by the silence before it was a foot from his body.

The farmer's ears stretched for a noise—any noise. His ears were ringing slightly and he pressed his hands over them, trying to make it stop.

Then the roaring and clacking sound came again, swirling through the silence but not eclipsing it. The farmer staggered to the window, expecting the roof to come off at any second, ripping him and his missus into the gaping maw of the cyclone. What he saw was more terrifying than a storm.

Surrounding his cabin was a band of shadow figures, circling and whirling like autumn leaves. They wailed into the deadened silence. Each individual voice was faint and tinny, but together they made the cyclone sound that first woke him. Red witch lights appeared and disappeared among the shadowy band. Every revolution of the massive circle brought the spirits a foot closer to the house. It would not be long before the ha'nts burst through the walls and claimed the lives of the farmer and his missus.

"It's the spirits of them old skulls," the farmer gasped. "They've come to get me!"

The wails of the dead grew louder. Red spirit lights flashed brighter than fireworks. The farmer clapped his hands to his head, afraid the screeching would drive him mad. He dropped to his knees and started praying, hoping the holy words would keep the ha'nts at bay.

The unearthly roar continued until first light rimmed the horizon. When at last it faded, the fearful farmer staggered to his feet and ran outside to the shed. He piled the sacks full of skulls into his cart and brought them straight back to the cave, where he laid them out all respectful and proper. Then he blocked up the entrance with brush and stones so his hound dog couldn't get in and steal any more bones.

When he got home, the farmer found his missus cooking breakfast with the hound dog begging for scraps at her feet. He gave a sigh of relief when he realized everything was back to normal.

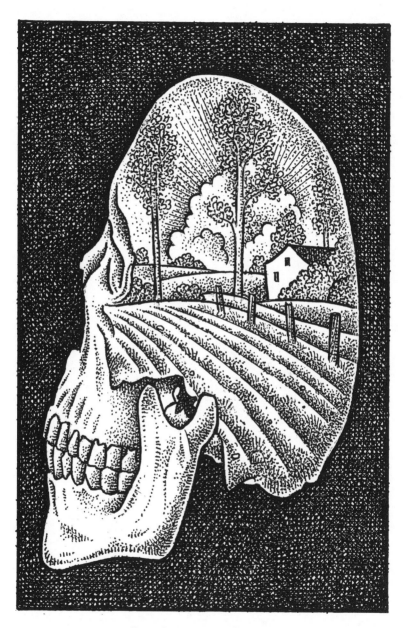

THE CAVERN OF SKULLS

His missus looked up from her cooking with a twinkling smile, still tickled that he'd bought her the special fertilizer. Then her eyes bulged, and she shouted: "What happened to ya? You've done gone old!"

The farmer stared at her blankly, then looked down at his hands. They were gnarled up and pitted with age. When he looked at his reflection in the mirror, he saw that his hair had turned snow white.

16

A Ghostly Slander

CHAPEL HILL

I sat with my back to the wall and my eye on the door as my nephew Lester, who was a clerk in my law office, wound his way through the crowd to the bar to order drinks for us. The usual patrons were scattered about the room, quaffing ale, playing cards, and throwing darts at a board.

My eye was caught by the vexed face of Peter Shand, the smith's hammerman, sitting at the next table. Mr. Shand was not my favorite citizen. In his youth, he had a habit of wreaking vengeance upon his young friends over any small slight or difference of opinion. A dropped cup of water had resulted in a black eye for my nephew, one long-ago day when both boys were in grammar school. Lester and Shand had forgotten the incident, but I never had. As an adult, Shand was more subtle in his punishments, but I found this made him more dangerous, not less. I wondered who had roused his ire this time. Then Lester returned with two brimming mugs of ale and I forgot the matter.

We were enjoying a second round of drinks when several rowdies joined Shand's table and pestered him for details about his soured relationship with the lovely Mysie Brown. Lester and I ceased our discussion of a baffling lawsuit in a neighboring town to eavesdrop. We knew and liked the lovely widow, who was a near neighbor with a lively intellect that ensured her family's survival after her husband disappeared. Mysie started selling milk and other sundries to support herself and her two children and made such a success of her business that she now owned a large farm and a plump bank account. She was highly sought-after by the bachelor population, and town gossip paired her with one after another man, but I had never seen her favor anyone. It was my private opinion that she still mourned her lost husband.

For the last several months, Peter Shand had been hanging around Mysie's place when he was done working at the smithy. The widow was paying him to do several heavy chores like digging fence posts and slaughtering the hogs. Rumor immediately paired the two, and folks talked of a spring wedding if things continued thus. Mysie stoutly denied the rumors, but the local gossips laughed off her protests. In their mind, the marriage was a settled thing. But Shand's stern countenance this evening indicated that the gossips had got it wrong again. I sat back and listened to his story.

"She seemed like such a nice woman," Shand said, shaking his head as he gazed into his drink. "But I was warned off, you see."

The men at his table scoffed. As hammerman to the blacksmith, Shand was the tallest and strongest of anyone in town, only excepting the smith himself. No other bachelor stood a chance against him in a fight. "No, lads, it wasn't the competition," Shand said. He glanced about and pretended to lower his voice, though I noted that his faux-whisper reached the far edges of the room. "'Twas a ghostly visitation."

The men reared back in their seats, faces shocked. One young lad grew pale and gulped the remainder of his ale in a single long swallow. Shand continued. "'Twas Saturday evening, and I had departed from the Widow Brown's place after fixing the fence. It was a fine moonlit night, so I stopped to smoke my pipe in that open patch near the quarry."

His listeners nodded in understanding. Shand's landlady did not allow smoking in her boardinghouse.

"When I checked my pockets, I realized that I didn't have a match," Shand continued. "At that moment, I looked up and saw a wispy-looking fellow drifting in and out of the moon shadows on the road. I called out: 'Good sir, do you have a match on you?' But the fellow didn't answer me. He walked toward the quarry as if he hadn't heard me, though I spoke loud and clear. I figured the man was deaf, so I stepped lively after him and repeated my question."

Lester and I exchanged knowing glances. In the Shand lexicon, this meant he planned to bully a match out of the man.

Shand said: "The man turned toward me, and to my shock I recognized the face of Jock Brown! I stopped in my tracks and cried: 'Good lord, man. I thought you were dead.' And then I realized that I could see the rim of the quarry right through his body! That's when I realized it was a ghost that was glaring at me in the moonlight."

Almost everyone in the barroom shuddered at this pronouncement.

I frowned. Ghost were a figment of the imagination. What was the hammerman up to?

Shand continued: "Jock Brown's feet floated a few inches off the ground, and his whole body started to glow. He cried:

111

'Do not marry Mysie or you will rue it all the days of your life. She is a base and black-hearted woman! You've been warned!' His voice raised chills up and down my spine. Before I could ask him what he meant by his warning, Jock Brown floated through the quarry fence and plummeted downward, vanishing under the black pool of water at the bottom. I rushed after him and looked down into the pit, but there was nary a ripple on the water to show where he'd been. I tell you, lads, my legs were shaking so bad that I barely made it back to the rooming house. And I haven't seen Mysie since that day."

Whispers ran through the room as everyone speculated what the ghost meant by warning Shand away from the widow. Was she a witch? A loose woman? What evil had she done that her dead husband had come back to scare away her suitor?

I tossed money on the table and beckoned to Lester. This story did not bode well for Mysie Brown or her dairy business. We hurried from the bar and headed directly to our neighbor's house to warn her.

Mysie sat drumming her fingers nervously against the kitchen table when I concluded the tale.

"That scoundrel," she said finally, looking first at me and then Lester. "He asked me to marry him last week and I told him I did not intend to marry anyone. I am doing just fine by myself, and anyway, he was only courting me because he wants my money and my property. Shand is trying to ruin me with this story."

I had come to the same conclusion.

"What recourse do I have? Can I sue him for libel?" Mysie asked.

"No, ma'am, for who would you accuse?" Lester said quietly. "Shand was just quoting the 'ghost' and you cannot sue a specter."

"But Shand made up the ghost," Mysie cried in exasperation. "Ghosts do not exist."

"First you would have to prove Shand was lying by proving there was no ghost. Then you might have a case against him. And how do you prove the lack of a ghost?" I asked.

Mysie covered her face in frustrated acceptance of my words. "What am I to do?" she asked in a muffled voice.

"Stay calm and deny all accusations. Act amused, as if sensible people would not believe such a story. Lester and I will also do our best to lay the rumors to rest," I said.

"It will not be enough," Mysie predicted grimly, before thanking us and seeing us to the door.

She was right, of course. Shand had been very clever in his approach. Not everyone believed his ghostly tale, but the gossip did enough damage that the widow's milk sales declined, and townsfolks started avoiding her.

Mysie Brown kept her head and continued treating everyone as kindly as before. The skeptical approach to the rumors taken by me, the local doctor, and the minister kept things from spiraling out of control, but it was an uncomfortable time for Mysie and her children, who were teased mercilessly at school.

About a month later, Shand staggered into the bar, clothing and hair askew and started raving about a second encounter with the ghost. According to the hammerman, Jock Brown's apparition rose up from the quarry, seized him by the throat and shook him so hard his teeth rattled. "I demand justice," the ghost howled. "Mysie struck me in the head and dumped my body into the pool at the bottom of the quarry. She must pay for her crime!" The horrified hearers of Shand's story sent immediately for the sheriff, who promised to look into the matter.

As soon as she heard of Shand's latest treachery, Mysie begged me to represent her interests. So the next day, when the sheriff dragged the quarry pool in search of Jock Brown's body, I was one of the witnesses who saw him pull a skeleton out of the water. My heart sank, for this seemed to support the ghostly claim, though I wondered at how easily the skeleton was found and how advanced its decomposition, for not a shred of skin or clothing was left. Jock Brown hadn't been gone that long. Nevertheless, the local doctor said it was a male skeleton and about the right age for the missing husband.

The story was in all the local papers. Mysie steadfastly proclaimed her innocence, but no one believed her. The minister preached against wickedness, and the local doctor told me in confidence that he could not say one way or another if the skeleton was truly Jock Brown. There was no sign of a head injury, and no way to tell if the man had drowned. The Sheriff brought Mysie into his office to examine her, with me present, but her tale remained consistent and there was no actual proof that the skeleton was her deceased husband. He didn't have enough evidence to arrest her, but that didn't stop the townsfolk from believing in her guilt. They kept pestering her to confess every time she appeared in public.

By this time, I thought the best thing for Mysie to do was to sell out and move away.

"And what if I do?" she asked me bitterly over a hot cup of tea at her kitchen table. "You know the story will follow me, even if I change my name. Somebody always recognizes you. Someone always remembers. Besides, the Sheriff asked to examine me again tomorrow. I may very well be hanged by the end of the year, just because I rejected an unwanted suitor."

I nodded and kept silent. She was right and I felt helpless to do anything for her. What use was a law degree in these circumstances?

Promptly at 3:00 p.m. the next day, Mysie and I appeared in the sheriff's office. He went patiently through each of the accusations, and she steadfastly—if brokenly—continued to deny and debunk every rumor. It was agonizing to watch. Just then I caught a glimpse through the window of my nephew Lester escorting a diminutive man up the front walkway. My eyes widened. A moment later, a perfunctory knock heralded the entrance of the small man. The sheriff looked up and gasped. Mysie reeled back in her chair, face as white as a sheet.

"Do you know me?" the man demanded of the sheriff.

Before the man could nod his affirmation, Mysie sprang out of the chair and threw herself upon the newcomer. "Jock, oh Jock! You're alive. You're home!" She clutched him frantically and burst into tears.

Jock Brown looked abashed and patted her awkwardly on the shoulder. Over her muffled sobs, he answered the sheriff's questions. No, he was not dead or knocked on the head or abducted. No, he had not been haunting the neighborhood accusing his wife of evil behavior. He had been living for the last several years in Raleigh, working as a tailor. Yes, he had quarreled with his wife, and had decided to separate from her, but he had known nothing of the murder accusation until Lester spotted him while visiting the capitol on business and demanded that he return and make things right.

"Why didn't you show the sheriff the letter I left you?" Jock asked his tearful wife.

"You left me a letter?" Mysie asked incredulously, lifting her head from his shoulder. "I never found a letter."

Jock Brown shook his head. "You must have. I put it on the kitchen table, in plain view. It was under the yellow jug."

"The yellow jug was broken the day you left," Mysie exclaimed. "The goat got into the house that morning. It knocked over the kitchen table and broke several pieces of crockery, including the jug. Then it ate every blessed thing in the kitchen, including my apron. It must have eaten the letter too." Mysie shook her head. "I never knew what happened to you. We searched for weeks after you vanished. I didn't put on widow's mourning for three months."

Jock paled. "I'm sorry, Mysie. I thought you knew."

I stepped forward. "For the record, sir, would you tell us what was in the letter? What was your quarrel about that you should form so desperate a resolve to leave wife and children? Was it anything deadly?"

Jock Brown looked embarrassed. "Salted porridge," he said.

I blinked. "I beg your pardon?"

"Mysie salted the porridge every morning," he explained sheepishly. "I hate salted porridge. I asked her over and again to make it another way, and she said this was the way her mother made it, and I could accept it or leave. So, I . . . left."

There was a stunned silence. Before we could recover, the doctor and the minister burst in to see the resurrected Jock Brown for themselves. Hard on their heels came my clever

A Ghostly Slander

nephew, who, having successfully collared the salted porridge gourmand, now produced a gravedigger who had employed Peter Shand to restore a vault full of skeletons during some recent cemetery alterations and had recently noticed that one skeleton was missing.

A group of furious townspeople hunted down the hammersmith, who was hiding in a barn, and gave him a good ducking in the quarry pool where he had pulled his malicious prank. Shand disappeared soon afterward, before the Browns could sue him for libel.

Jock Brown moved back in with his missus and children and set up a new tailor shop in the center of town. The family had Lester and me to dinner a few weeks after the furor had died down, and I asked Jock if they had resolved the issue of the porridge.

"Well sir, after eating the flavorless porridge they have in the big city, I find that a bit of salt doesn't seem so bad," Jock said. "If my Mysie gets too heavy handed, I just add more milk, since we've plenty of that nowadays."

PART TWO

Powers of Darkness and Light

17

Boo-Hag

ELIZABETH CITY

You know how they say some folks are lucky at cards and some are lucky at love? Well, that fit Bobby Hansen to a T. He was the best poker player in the county, but somehow he couldn't find himself a bride. Oh, he proposed to several girls and even got accepted by a few. But they always got cold feet a day or two before the wedding, and it was bye-bye Bobby.

After the third time, Bobby was mighty discouraged, and his pa felt real sore for him. They worked together in the family grocery store, and Bobby would sometimes sit on top of the pickle barrel and tell his pa his woes. His pa always told him to hang in there, because a nice lady was on her way. Neither of them believed it, but it made both of them feel better to hear it said.

Well, the day after their latest talk, an old woman who poled her barge through the swamp to deliver milk and eggs to the grocery store had a long talk with Bobby's pa. It seemed she had this daughter who was hankering after a husband with a good steady job, and the old woman thought Bobby would do the job nicely. She suggested they introduce the pair at the next dance, and Bobby's pa agreed.

120

The night of the dance, Bobby's pa insisted that his son dress in his best. Bobby was dragging his feet a little, remembering all those women who played him false and not wanting to go, but his pa insisted. Well, the moment Bobby clapped eyes on the dark-eyed, red-lipped girl from the swamp, he was head over heels in love. Her eyes sparkled like the sunlight on the bay. Her skin was as creamy as new milk. Her voice was low and sweet.

The pair cuddled and cooed and waltzed the whole night long. Come sunrise Bobby was all for bringing his new love before the visiting priest who delivered his sermons in the grocery store (since there weren't no church in that vicinity) and getting married right away. Well, the girl was willing to get married, but not by a priest.

"Let's just go to the city and have the judge marry us," she said to Bobby, and he was so smitten that he agreed, though it would have been quicker and easier to walk a mile down the road to see the priest.

By the next evening they were wed, and Bobby brought his pretty bride to the little cottage he rented just down the road from the family grocery. It had a nice front porch with a swing, a big bedroom on the second floor, and a big attic with a window that could be made up into a second guestroom should his new mother-in-law care to visit from her home in the swamp.

After fixing him a nice dinner, Bobby's new bride sat awhile in the rocking chair near their bed while Bobby yawned and watched her fondly. She cuddled under the blanket and knitted and hummed while Bobby's eyes grew real heavy and he nodded off. He didn't wake up until early morning, when his new bride crept into bed all hot and sweaty and fell asleep at once. When he asked her where she'd been, she wouldn't answer him. Bobby was mighty sore that his bride had snuck out on him on their wedding night, but she got snappish, and her eyes blazed when he questioned her, so he backed down.

Life took on an odd pattern for Bobby. During the day everything was perfect. His wife was sweet and pretty and loving. She kept the house sparkling clean and cooked him wonderful meals. But each night she refused to come to bed after supper. Like their wedding night, she sat up singing and rocking and knitting until he was asleep, and she did not come to bed till just before dawn. She was always sweaty and cranky when she came to bed, and she went to sleep before Bobby could question her.

Bobby was very confused and upset by this behavior and finally confided in his pa one morning after opening up the grocery store. Bobby's pa was awful worried. The visiting priest had gone on to his next parish, and there was no one else they could consult about the matter except the local conjure woman. So Bobby's pa sent him to her with a couple of chickens as a gift.

The conjure woman knew all about hoodoo magic and was an excellent herbalist. Local folks went to her when they were sick, on account of the doctor lived nigh on twenty miles away. When she heard Bobby's story, she told him to pretend to go to sleep that night and watch what his new bride did. Then he was to come back and tell her everything. Bobby agreed.

The next evening, he pretended to fall asleep while his bride rocked and sang in her chair. Then he followed her up to the attic and watched through the crack in the open door as she sat down at the spinning wheel and spun off her skin, leaving only pulsing red muscles and blue veins. She was a terrifying sight as she sprang through the window and flew away into the night.

Boo-Hag

Bobby ran out to the privy and was sick after he saw her. Who—what—was this monster he had married? He was still trembling with shock when his bride, looking like a normal person again, crept into bed at dawn, and he had trouble behaving normally at breakfast.

As soon as he could get away, Bobby ran to the home of the conjure woman and told her about the spinning wheel and the terrible skinless creature who flew away from his attic. "A boo-hag," the conjure woman said at once. "You've married a boo-hag."

"What's a boo-hag?" asked Bobby.

"A boo-hag is a witch and a shape-shifter," said the conjure woman. "She lures men into her trap and then delivers them to her boo-daddy, who eats their flesh and gnaws their bones. And that's what she'll do to you if you don't get rid of her first."

Then the conjure woman told Bobby exactly what he needed to do to get rid of the boo-hag. There were two facts, she said, about boo-hags that—when known—could rescue a man from her trap. The first fact was that a boo-hag couldn't fly through a window or door that was painted blue. The second fact was that if a boo-hag didn't get back into her skin before dawn, she would be trapped without it and never again able to disguise herself as a human. So if Bobby got himself some blue paint and spread it on every window frame and every door frame, then the boo-hag could not enter his house and come dawn would be revealed for the monstrous creature she was. However, if Bobby wanted to be rid of the creature entirely, then he should leave one tiny window unpainted and keep it open a sliver so the boo-hag could squeeze through. Then he was to fill up her skin with salt and pepper, which would burn her up from the inside

123

out. By the time she found the unpainted window, the boo-hag would be forced to hurry into her skin or forfeit her human disguise. She wouldn't have time to notice the trap he'd set for her until it was too late!

Bobby promised to do exactly as the conjure woman said. That night, Bobby lingered over his dinner, looking with sad eyes at the pretty woman sitting opposite him. He knew she was really a monster inside, but it was so nice to have a little wife in his home. He hated like anything to see her go. But he didn't want to get eaten by a boo-daddy, and that was his fate if she stayed. So he went up to their bedroom and pretended to fall asleep while she rocked and sang and knitted. Then he followed her quietly upstairs and put salt and pepper into her skin after her ugly, red-muscled, blue-veined figure had flown out the window to her boo-daddy. He spent the rest of the night painting over every door and window frame with blue paint, leaving only one small unpainted window open in the cellar. He nailed it up so that it would open no further than a crack, just as the conjure woman instructed him. Then he hid himself behind a large chest of drawers up in the attic to wait for the boo-hag.

Just before dawn the boo-hag flew up to the attic window. As soon as she touched the blue frame, she gave a shriek of pain and rage. Bobby listened as she flew around the house, testing each window and door and howling like a banshee when it burned her skinless hands. Then she found the little window in the cellar, and he heard the thump as she landed beside it, followed by a painful whimpering sound as she squeezed and squeezed herself through the narrow opening, her skinless red muscles and blue veins tearing painfully against the rough wood.

Boo-Hag

The boo-hag ran up three flights of stairs into the attic and squeezed and squeezed into her skin as fast as she could. She barely got it on when the first light of dawn shone over the horizon. And that was when the salt and pepper did their work, burning the boo-hag's body from the inside out. With a scream of agony, she flung herself out the attic window. Glass shattered everywhere as she tried to fly away, tearing at her skin to get it off. But it was too late. She exploded into tiny pieces right over the swamp, and the fish had a mighty feast of cooked boo-hag for breakfast that morning.

So Bobby was once again without a wife. But bachelorhood looked much better to him after his brief marriage, and he never went looking for a woman again. 'Course, after he made a pile of money in gold and minerals, the girls started chasing him. But that's another story.

18

The Coffin

Bang! Bang! Bang!

The sharp sound roused me from sleep at 3:00 a.m., according to the chiming of the grandfather clock in the hall. I sat up, startled by the noise.

Bang! Bang! Bang!

I heard the sound again. This time my befuddled head made sense of the noise. It was the sound of someone banging a nail with a hammer. And it was coming from the shop next door. From *my* carpenter shop, in fact!

I shook my wife, Lizzie, awake and said, "Honey! Somebody's in the shop. I'm going to see who it is, and *howdy boy*, are they going to be in trouble when I get through with them!"

Lizzie sat up sleepily.

"It's probably some fool kids messing about," she said as I struggled into my britches. "I'd better check on the baby. If them fool kids woke her up after it took me three ages to get her to sleep, they're gonna feel the edge of my tongue!"

From the workshop next door came the thump of heavy wood being moved about, and then a very loud sawing noise.

127

Tossing my nightcap on the bed, I struggled into my shirt and ran downstairs to get my rifle while Lizzie checked on our two-year-old daughter. I filled it with rock salt, which stings like the dickens and gets the point across without actually hurting anybody. Then I was out the front door and running toward my shop.

First thing I noticed: It was dark in there. Way too dark for someone to be messing about with hammer and saw unless they was aiming to injure themselves. I slowed down to a trot, wondering what was going on. For a moment, the shop was silent. Then the bang-bang-banging of the hammer started again. I could hear it clearly coming from the carpenter shop, though there was nothing to see. I squinted at the shop, puzzled and a bit frightened. Then I perceived a faint blue glow and smiled grimly to myself. Aha! I headed for the door, my gun ready to "persuade" any kids messing around inside to leave be and go home.

I yanked the door open. There was no one inside. At least no one visible. Instead, I saw a glowing blue coffin laid out on sawhorses in the center of the shop. A hammer hovered over it. As I watched, it started banging another nail into place. Then the saw rose up and started cutting another board to the proper size to fit the side of the coffin.

I gasped, my heart banging even harder than the hammer. Cold chills ran up the outside of my arms, and all my muscles froze. What was this uncanny thing? My stomach started flip-flopping inside my gut, and the hairs on my scalp prickled. In that moment little details sprang out at me. The coffin was made of cedar. It cast no shadow on the floor. The hammer was a new one I had never seen before. I could see the outline of my saw resting on the bench, and yet somehow it was also hovering in the air, teeth sawing into the phantom board.

Suddenly, the light went out, and the coffin vanished along with the floating hammer and saw. My heart gave a painful stutter, and my legs unfroze. With a terrified shriek, I staggered backward out the door, clutching my rifle.

"Haints! We're being hainted!" I raced back to the house, put my gun on the rack over the door, and ran upstairs to the bedroom to tell Lizzie what I'd seen in the shop. Lizzie's eyes got real big as she listened, and she clutched the quilt up to her chin as I told her about the glowing coffin.

"That ain't haints, Jed," she said to me. "That there's a premonition, that's what it is. Somebody's gonna die, and your gonna build them a cedar coffin for the buryin'. I'm sure of it."

I hadn't thought of that. I sank down on the edge of the bed. "My great-granny up in Nova Scotia calls them forerunners," I said thoughtfully. "Lights and sounds and visions ya see jest before a person passes. I dint think we got 'em here in the Carolinas."

"People get 'em everywhere," said Lizzie. "There ain't nothing you can do 'bout that premonition now, Jed, so come to bed."

She was right, of course. I sighed and slipped under the covers. But it took me a long time to go to sleep.

I weren't too surprised the next morning when we got word that Lizzie's aunt had passed in the night. It was 3:00 a.m. when she died, the same hour we'd heard the ghostly noises in the carpenter shop. Lizzie's uncle James stopped by the house to give us the sad news, and he asked me to build a coffin for his wife out of cedar, her favorite tree. To thank me for my trouble,

The Coffin

he went out and bought me a brand-new hammer for the shop. It was the same one I'd seen floating in the air over the glowing coffin. I nearly dropped it when he first handed it to me.

It felt plumb awkward setting out the sawhorses and cutting up the boards that day. I kept remembering how I'd sort of seen myself doing it last night, and the thought made my hands shake. But someone had to make a coffin out of respect for Lizzie's aunt that passed.

I made the prettiest cedar coffin I could with all sorts of fancy scrollwork, and I polished it up good so you could see your face in the wood. Uncle James was s'pleased with that coffin. It did his wife proud, he said. But I could hardly bear to look at it. It didn't feel right to me, as if seeing the glowing coffin in my shop had somehow made me responsible for the death of Lizzie's aunt. Which my wife said was nonsense.

Maybe so. But I never went out to investigate any more mysterious noises coming from my shop. I'd had enough of premonitions to last me a lifetime.

19

The Honeymoon

GREAT SMOKY MOUNTAINS NATIONAL PARK

Mary was thrilled to pieces when George Bolton came a-courting. He was jest about the handsomest man in the mountains—bold, daring, fierce. He was also a good hunter and a good farmer who would be able to provide for a family. And it was awful cute the way he'd run his hands through his dark curls, turn bright red, and stammer when he talked to her. He spent a lot of time staring at his own feet and mumbling when he first started walking her home from church, and he was red as a beet the first evening he came a-sparking to her parents' house. They'd sat on the porch and drank lemonade as the spicy air of the hot summer evening drowsed around them.

After that, George came around most evenings to talk to Mary or bring her presents: a whistle pig he'd shot in the woods, some wild roses he'd found in a clearing, some pretty stones to put in her rock garden. By the end of summer, Mary's mama claimed she was floatin' instead of walkin', and no one was surprised when George proposed marrying around Christmastime. It was the only way they'd get any sense out of Mary, her papa claimed, tapping his girl on the chin. Mary jest grinned at him and kept a tight hold of George's hand.

George spent most of the autumn season constructing a new cabin for his Mary. He found a place in a shady holler on the mountain that was protected from the mountain wind by a tall stand of trees. The holler had a cool, bubbling spring at its center that they could use for water. It was a perfect place for a cabin. The view from the front door, looking out over the valley through a gap in the trees, would be magnificent. And there was a huge flat rock on the ground he could use for both hearthstone and floor. It was pocked with small holes, but his Mary wouldn't mind those, and it made the cabin seem rather posh to have a stone floor.

George finished the cabin around Thanksgiving and carefully shut it up to await the coming of his bride. George and Mary were married at the church the day after Christmas, to a great whooping and hollering and carrying on by their many siblings and cousins and friends. George's brothers threatened to serenade the newlyweds in the middle of the night, and George threatened to knock their blocks off if they did. Though that wouldn't discourage them in the least, Mary remarked as George helped her up into the rough farm wagon he'd borrowed from a neighbor for this ceremonious occasion.

George drove Mary up to the cabin in the light of the swiftly setting sun and showed her around her new home. The one-room cabin had a big loft overhead; there were beehives out back that were going to make their fortune in honey sales; a newly dug privy stood back by the trees; and, of course, the bubbling spring was only a few feet from the front door. Mary oohed and aahed over every detail, and they sat on the door stoop, snuggling together and admiring the view until the sun set behind the mountains and it grew too dark to see.

Then George carried his bride over the threshold, gave her a gosh-almighty big kiss on the lips that made her giggle and blush happily, and went to build a roaring fire in their new grate. After cooking some dinner, the happy honeymooners retired to bed and cuddled together under the thick eiderdown.

"Yer brothers are gonna come serenading us sometime tonight," Mary told her new husband sleepily.

"Yep. No doubt," George mumbled, already nodding off in the warmth of the fire.

Mary smiled and curled herself a little closer to her new husband. In a few moments they were both asleep.

They were both awakened abruptly out of a deep sleep by a slimy, slithery, hissing sort of sound that was getting louder by the minute. "Is that yer brothers?" Mary asked, rolling over and rubbing her eyes. "I expected them to play the banjo at least!"

"I ain't sure what it is," George said. "I'll build up the fire, and we can check."

George slipped out of bed, his feet hitting the pocked stone floor, which was still warm from the blaze they'd made earlier. He walked toward the glowing coals in the fireplace, one step, two. And his foot landed on something squirmy and round and scaly. A snake! It hissed and rattled at him, and he became aware suddenly that the dark floor was alive with hissing rattlesnakes. They writhed all around his feet and legs, and he felt the horrible sting as their fangs struck his bare legs over and over.

"Rattlers!" George gasped desperately to his bride. "They must have been sleeping under the stone and come up through the holes when they sensed the heat of the fire! Get under that eiderdown right now, Mary! Right now! Cover yerself up and *don't move!*"

George could feel poison filling up his body. He staggered another step—he didn't really know where he wanted to go anymore or why. The snakes were climbing his body . . . or perhaps he had fallen down among them. His body was ablaze with pain, and he felt so tired. So tired . . .

Mary, sobbing softly in horror and fear, slid underneath the thick eiderdown and lay very, very still. She heard George moving for a few moments more. Then there was silence save for the slithering, rattling, and hissing of the snakes. Several times during that endless night, she felt snakes sliding back and forth over the eiderdown, and one large snake seemed to have taken up residence across her feet. She didn't dare move.

Just before dawn, there came the crashing sound of saucepans being banged together right outside the window. Mary jumped at the sound, but the snakes didn't notice the tiny movement she made under the eiderdown. They had stopped moving around so much once the temperature inside the cabin had cooled down. The tinny sound of a bugle being played poorly accompanied the slamming saucepans, and then somebody kicked in with a banjo. Mary could hear her brothers-in-law singing a bawdy song. Somebody knocked on the front door and then banged it open. She heard her brothers-in-law march over the doorsill with their heavy boots and then heard them gasp in horror, the song abruptly grinding to a halt as all three of them saw the bloated body of their brother George lying on the floor, surrounded by rattlers grown sluggish in the chilly morning air.

One of the men, seeing the lump on the bed, called: "Hang on, Mary! We're coming." Then the men set to work, grimly killing snake after snake and tossing the bodies in the

THE HONEYMOON

corner. When it was safe, they pulled Mary out from under the eiderdown, surprised and relieved to find her alive. But the ordeal had turned her lovely golden curls snow white, and her face was ever afterward lined with wrinkles like those of a woman twice her age. The cabin was closed up forever, and Mary went back home to live with her folks.

These days, if anyone chances to walk near that old holler at night, they will often hear sounds coming from the derelict cabin with the pocked stone floor. Despairing shouts, the hiss and rattle of snakes, and, clear as day, a man's voice shouting: "Don't move, Mary. *Don't move!*"

20

The Carpenter

BAT CAVE

J. J. Tucker owned a big farm just south of Bat Cave, and he was just about as prosperous as a man could be. All his horses and cows were plump and fit, his barns were watertight and filled with hay and grain for the winter, and his wife was pleasant and downright pretty to boot. J. J.'s only sorrow was for his little boy, Arnie, who'd had a crippled leg ever since he fell off the wagon and got run over by a wheel.

J. J. Tucker had a generous heart toward most every person he met. If any passing peddler stopped at his gate, he'd purchase some of his wares, whether needed or not. Anyone down on their luck would soon find a dollar in their pockets, courtesy of J. J. Tucker, and could sit down to a good meal made by his missus anytime they felt a mite hungry. He gave generously to the church and was right up on the roof with the other men helping with repairs after a big storm.

Considering his big heart and generous spirit, folks considered it strange that J. J. and his next-door neighbor—once the best of friends—were no longer on speaking terms. But Ted Franklin and J. J. Tucker had argued strenuously over the ownership of the property that lay between their farms, and in the end they'd stopped speaking to each other. Worse, Ted Franklin dug a deep ditch between the two properties and diverted a small stream into it to further separate the once-friendly neighbors, one from the other.

Not long after the ditch was dug, a stranger came strolling up the lane toward J. J. Tucker's farm. J. J., just done with the morning milking, came to the gate to meet him, all smiles. J. J. greeted the man gladly, and the stranger said, "I'm a carpenter looking for a day's work. Someone told me you might have a job for me."

J. J. beamed with delight. "I do indeed," he said, opening the farm gate wide and inviting the carpenter through.

J. J. led the carpenter to the footpath that once joined his farm with his neighbor's. "See that stream over there," he said to the carpenter. "My neighbor Ted dug that stream after we had a falling-out over some land. Now I aim to do him one better. I'd like you to build a big fence right along the edge of that ditch so he can't see my farm anymore. There's poles and fencing in the barn just here. Think you can do it?"

The carpenter studied the situation for a moment. "I think I can build something you'd like," he said at last.

"Capital!" said J. J. Tucker. "I'll nip to the upper field after breakfast to chop some weed. Meantime, come break bread with us!" The carpenter smiled and accepted the breakfast invitation.

Little Arnie was quite taken with the carpenter when J. J. brought him to the house. The little boy talked and talked excitedly during the meal, and he watched from the window when the man headed down the footpath with his toolbox.

"Mama, can I watch the carpenter work?" he pleaded, limping around to face his plump mother, who was busy kneading bread at the large kitchen table.

"If he says you can," said his fond mother. "But don't talk his ear off like you did at breakfast."

Little Arnie grinned and promised his mother before maneuvering slowly out the door with his crutch. Dragging his twisted leg behind him, he limped slowly down the footpath, the crutch thumping in the dirt. He stopped a few feet from where the carpenter was working and asked if he could watch for a while. The man looked up with a smile so sweet and tender that Little Arnie's heart swelled with joy. "Of course you may," the carpenter said, and Little Arnie sat down on a stump to watch the man sawing boards to the proper length and then nailing them to the frame.

All day long the carpenter worked as Little Arnie sat and watched. The carpenter had a splendid voice and sang many songs for the delighted child. He was also a storyteller and told Arnie wonderful tales about faraway places and interesting people.

At noon, Missus Tucker brought them a basket of fried chicken to eat, and they supped together, the best of pals. The day sped by on wings. Little Arnie could not remember when he had enjoyed himself so much.

The carpenter finished his work just before supper. He cleaned up the job site and then walked back to the house easy and slow, so the little boy could keep up without hurting his twisted leg. So kindly was this done that Little Arnie never realized that the carpenter had slowed his customary pace to accommodate him.

As they reached the house, J. J. Tucker bustled out with a huge smile. "Done then?" he asked jovially.

"Done, indeed. Come see," said the carpenter.

As the men turned back toward the footpath, the carpenter stopped a moment and laid his hand on Little Arnie's head. He smiled down at the child. "Go in to your mother now, and leave your crutch by the door when you go in," he said. "Thank you for the company today."

"You're welcome," the little boy said happily, turning toward the door.

The carpenter and J. J. walked down the footpath together, and a moment later, J. J. stopped dead in the center of the trail. A beautifully sculpted bridge spanned the stream in the place where he had asked the carpenter to construct a fence. And crossing the bridge, hand outstretched in delighted greeting, was Ted Franklin! Before J. J. could process what had happened, indeed, before he could even exclaim in surprise, his neighbor had seized his right hand and was pumping it up and down.

"Bless you, J. J. Bless you ten times over," Ted cried. "I was miserable after I dug that ditch. I wanted us to be friends again, but somehow I could never bring myself to say so. Now you've built this bridge to join our land together again, and I can't thank you enough!"

Finally regaining his voice, J. J. said, "I've wanted to be friends too. But I was too proud to say so. Much as I'd like to claim credit for the bridge, it was the carpenter here who built the bridge."

The neighbors both turned and beamed upon the carpenter, who heaved his toolbox up onto his shoulder and nodded at them. Then he vanished.

THE CARPENTER

The men gasped and reeled back on their heels in astonishment. Where had the carpenter gone?

At that very moment, there came a shout of "Daddy" from the direction of the house. The neighbors turned and looked toward the house, just as Little Arnie came pelting down the footpath. He was running as fast as ever a boy could run; his twisted leg had been made whole again the instant he had laid his crutch by the door.

Little Arnie threw himself into his father's arms. Tears rolling down his cheeks, J. J. swept his son up and shouted: "Praise be! Oh, praise be!"

The two neighbors exchanged a look over Little Arnie's head and then glanced as one toward the bridge.

"He healed a child and built a bridge," Ted murmured thoughtfully. "I wonder . . ."

Hugging his little boy tight, J. J. smiled at his neighbor and said, "Perhaps we should just say: Thank God for the carpenter."

"Amen," Ted said heartily. "Amen."

21

Doppelgänger

WATAUGA COUNTY

By the time the doctor left the house, it was only an hour or so before dawn. He was weary almost beyond bearing, for the birth had taken nearly twenty-four hours, but the good master of the house and his lady now had a healthy pair of twins who were bawling mightily for food when the doctor departed.

"Come, Gray. Let's go home," the doctor sighed, saddling up his patient gray horse. Gray turned calm eyes on his old friend and nuzzled the doctor's face, knocking his hat awry. The doctor smiled and patted the horse on the nose.

Swinging wearily into the saddle, the doctor rode out of the farmyard and into the dark lane. "I'm getting too old for this kind of life, Gray," the doctor said to his horse as they clip-clopped down the farm lane toward the main road. The horse snorted as if in answer to the doctor's words. The doctor laughed and said, "It's true. My father dropped dead when he was sixty-two, and I turned sixty-two last week." The doctor sighed heavily and was silent for a few moments as they turned onto the main road, heading toward Boone.

"They say," the doctor continued aloud after a few minutes of plodding, "that Father saw his doppelgänger a few days

144

before he passed. Do you know what a doppelgänger is, Gray?" He reached forward and patted his horse on the neck. Gray tossed his head a bit, perking his ears back to show his old friend that he was listening.

"I wasn't sure myself, so I looked it up when I heard the story from Mother. A doppelgänger is a ghostly double of yourself. To see yourself repeated thus is an omen of death." The doctor shook his head, white hair slipping out from under the hat to flop across his forehead. Weary to his bones, he fell silent again. It was hard work to sit upright against the gentle swaying of Gray's back.

The woods around them were filled with the soft rustles of foxes and other night creatures searching for food. The crickets sang softly, and once an owl hooted right overhead, startling the doctor and Gray. Occasionally, the doctor would catch a glimpse of the starry sky between the leaves overhead, and here and there shafts of pure-white moonlight pierced the dark canopy and created lovely beams that illuminated the road ahead.

"Mother told me that Father walked out on the front porch one morning and saw himself walking up the front path," the doctor said to Gray as they entered a beam of moonlight. For a moment doctor and horse glowed white, as if they had turned into ghostly doubles. "The doppelgänger went right past Father and through the front door, but when Father followed it inside, it was gone." They stepped out of the moonbeam into the shadows and entered the Big Laurel—a section of the woods that was densely tangled with laurel ivy and other mountain timber. It was said to be haunted by the spirit of a headless dog, but the doctor and Gray had never seen it, and they rode this way nearly every day.

Ahead of them, the road made a hairpin turn around a giant fallen tree. There was a break in the canopy of laurel and timber where the giant tree had once been. The moonlight shone down through the break, illuminating the road on either side of the fallen tree. As the doctor drew closer to the moonbeam on this section of road, he realized—between one blink and the next—that a dark figure on horseback was approaching the moonbeam on the far side of the tree.

In the distance the church bell tolled out five times for 5:00 a.m. as the doctor and Gray stepped into the moonbeam together. The doctor glanced across the fallen tree and found himself staring at a man wearing a dark coat and hat, with a strand of white hair slipping down on his forehead. The man's face was a mirror of the doctor's, and his horse was a mirror of Gray.

The doctor's mouth dropped open. His heart stuttered and then began to thunder against his ribs in shock. Gray didn't appear to notice the ghostly visitation. He kept moving forward out of the moonbeam. As soon as they entered the shadowy bend that led to the far side of the log, the vision vanished. Then they rounded the hairpin bend, and the doctor could see the trembling moonbeam where the horseman had stood but a moment before. The moonbeam was empty. A moment later, Gray plowed right through it and kept going.

The doctor slumped forward, heart pounding and legs trembling visibly against the sides of his horse. Confused, Gray stopped, turning his ears back and forth, trying to understand what his old friend wanted him to do. The doctor drew in one ragged breath, then another. Slowly he sat up. "Walk on, Gray," he told his faithful steed, and the horse stepped forward obediently.

The doctor's heart rate was so high now that he felt dizzy and sick. As Gray approached the next farm lane, the doctor turned his old horse into it and went up to the house. The night was shifting into the gray dimness of early morning, and the doctor knew the farmer would be getting up to milk his cows. In fact, the farmer was just leaving through the side door of the house when the doctor fell off his horse at the gate. The farmer—an old acquaintance of the doctor's—hurried over to help him into the house. The good lady of the house thrust him into a chair, gave him a hot cup of tea dosed with whiskey, and cut him some bread and cheese to eat.

The whole family soon gathered around, and the doctor told everyone about the figure he'd seen in the Big Laurel at the bend in the road. He told them that the phantom rode a gray horse, but he could not bring himself to mention that he'd seen his own face on the horseman. Some things were meant to be private. Besides, he might be mistaken. He'd been thinking about doppelgängers and death omens all evening, and he was very tired from the birthing.

The farmer, seeing the doctor's weariness, had his eldest son drive the doctor home with old Gray tied behind the wagon. The doctor entered his front door shortly after dawn, pausing just long enough to give a weary wave to the cheerful boy who was leading Gray to the stable for him. His worried wife met him in the front hall and led him upstairs. As they mounted the steps, the doctor told his wife all about the vision he'd seen at the Big Laurel. He finished the tale as he stepped over the threshold of his bedroom. His weary eyes were on the warm comfort of the large bed he shared with his spouse when he felt a shooting pain in his arm that rose up and up until it encompassed his whole

DOPPELGÄNGER

body in one bright flash. The doctor fell heavily to the floor and did not hear his wife's scream.

For two days, the doctor lay in a coma after his massive heart attack. He died just before dawn on the third day, just as the church bell tolled out five times for 5:00 a.m.

22

Dreams and Visions

PINEOLA

Aunt Sally looked up from her spinning wheel with a smile when she heard the knock on her door. Aunt Sally loved company, and she'd been feeling a tad lonely that afternoon, what with everyone out in the fields working the harvest. She brushed off her apron, tidied her hair, and went to open the door. Standing there, hat in hand, was her nephew Blake.

"Well, Blake! Come on in," Aunt Sally cried happily. She pulled her nephew in the door, set him down at the table, and got him a drink of cider.

Blake smiled at his aunt over the rim of his cup and said, "My Betty's a mite nervous at spending the night alone in our cabin. She was wondering if you'd come stay with her while I'm away doing the rounds." Blake sold tinware for a living, and often he'd take to the road for five to ten days at a time to peddle his wares.

"I'd be happy to," Aunt Sally said, beaming with delight. "Let me pack up a few things, and we can go right now!"

Blake gave a sigh of relief. He didn't know what he'd do if Aunt Sally had said no. It wasn't just that Betty would fret. He was also worried about their neighbor Ralph, who had once sparked with Betty before she met Blake. Ralph was still interested in Blake's pretty wife, of that he was certain. What Blake didn't know was how his wife felt about her old beau. It worried him, because he was on the road a lot, and Betty got lonesome. Having Aunt Sally around would keep a lid on things, Blake was sure.

Betty greeted Aunt Sally with relief, and the two ladies were happily planning out their time together when Blake left on his rounds. They would work on Betty's new quilt, and Aunt Sally would spin while Betty knitted and would help harvest the honey from the beehives out back. And there were apples to pick and canning to do. The time would just speed past.

A few days into this promising agenda, Betty came down with a nasty cough, and Aunt Sally put her to bed with a mustard plaster. Then she settled down in a comfortable chair with her knitting and drowsed the evening away, rousing herself occasionally to put a log on the fire. Finally, she laughed to herself, wondering why she was bothering to stay up.

Aunt Sally went over to the bed where Betty lay sleeping and pulled the trundle bed from underneath it. But before she could step into it, the front door blew open with a crash, and a tall man, dark featured, with a horned head, hooves instead of feet, and a lashing tail stepped into the room and pointed a finger at Sally. Behind him, Sally could just see writhing, dancing figures—women, children, and black hellcats—against a backdrop of red flames.

"Beware," the devil-man called. "Beware!" Then the devil, the flames, and the dancers all vanished as suddenly as they arrived, and Sally found herself still kneeling next to the trundle bed in the flickering firelight, ready to crawl inside. Shaking

151

from head to toe, Aunt Sally dove under the covers and prayed for the Lord to spare her and Betty from evil. Finally, she fell into a disturbed sleep and woke unrefreshed in the morning.

Betty's cold had really taken hold by then, so Aunt Sally spent most of the day nursing her niece by marriage and working at the spinning wheel. When Betty fell asleep in the afternoon, Aunt Sally slipped outside to gather pine knots. She wanted a big bright fire in the hearth tonight in case that devil-man came back. The cabin was awful dark at night, and the pine knots would help illuminate the dark cabin and keep the devil from the door. At least Aunt Sally hoped they would. She put a great big pile of pine knots by the chimney and then went to tend Betty, who was stirring restlessly against the pillows.

Aunt Sally kept the fire blazing with pine knots all evening while Betty slept. Finally, she decided that the devil-man wasn't coming back. Sighing with relief, she crept over to the bed and pulled out the trundle. Immediately, the front door slammed open and the darkly wicked devil-man stepped inside, eyes blazing red like the flames silhouetting him. Aunt Sally could see the dancers again. She counted nine women, four children, and nine black hellcats.

As the devil advanced into the room, one of the black hellcats scrambled through the door and sprang into the fire, rolling happily about and batting at the pine knots. "Here, you. Get out of there," Aunt Sally scolded, forgetting the devil-man for a moment. She dearly loved cats—even black ones—and didn't want it to get burned. She strode over to the fire and glared down at the black cat. It yawned, rolled over on its back, and stared lazily up at her with amber eyes.

Aunt Sally sensed movement behind her. She whirled away from the fire and glared at the devil-man, who was standing over the bed with a vial of blood in his hand, dripping the blood down onto Betty's pretty white fingers.

"You! Stop that right now," Aunt Sally said, angry now. "Get out of here! Both of you. Right now." Seizing a blazing branch from the fire, she swatted at the black cat and then used it like a sword, feinting left and right at the devil. He laughed, pocketed the vial of blood, and calmly caught the blazing end of the branch in his hands. Then he bowed to Aunt Sally and vanished.

Once again, Aunt Sally found herself kneeling next to the trundle bed in the flickering firelight, ready to crawl inside. "Lord have mercy! It must be a vision of some kind," she muttered. "But I don't want to know what kind of vision has the devil in it!"

Grimly, Aunt Sally crawled into the trundle bed and said her prayers, begging the Lord to spare her and Betty from evil. But somehow she wasn't comforted by her prayers. She fell into a restless sleep and dreamed . . .

She dreamed of a dark night with no moon or stars. The fireplace was filled to the top with pine knots, but the light did not reach more than a foot beyond the hearth. And just outside the door came the sound of digging.

Aunt Sally rose slowly from the trundle bed and dragged one weary foot after another to the front door. She did not want to see what was outside, but something morbid and dark compelled her forward. She opened the door and stared outside at a group of men digging a grave, surrounded—oddly enough—by a flock of chickens. They had to keep shooing the chickens out of the open grave. To the right of the grave diggers, Aunt Sally saw a hand thrust forth out of the apple tree holding a white-handled knife. The knife began pruning away the small twigs from the tree, which tumbled to the ground beneath it.

Then Aunt Sally heard a grunting sound and the thud of hooves. Turning, she saw a big white ox with black spots walking up the trail toward the cabin. A man was riding the ox, but she couldn't see his face. Wondering what the knife wielder would do when it—he?—saw the ox rider, she turned to look at the apple tree. But the hand with the knife was gone, leaving only a number of pruned twigs on the ground. Bewildered, Aunt Sally turned again to the ox rider and saw the man lying flat on the ground, and the ox settling itself down on the ground next to the man, waiting patiently for its master to rise.

Then everything vanished and the world went dark . . .

And Aunt Sally awoke to the cheerful jingling of a wagonload of tinware coming up the trail toward the house. She'd overslept! Blake was almost home, and there was no breakfast on the table to greet him. Forgetting all about her dream, she woke Betty, who was feeling much better by now, and scurried about getting breakfast for her nephew.

It was only when Aunt Sally was back in her cozy cottage on her son's property that she remembered her visions and the dream that had followed them. Blood dripping on Betty's white fingers, the open grave, the white-handled knife, the spotted ox, and the devil-man saying, "Beware!"

About a week after she returned home, Aunt Sally opened the front door to let in some fresh air, and a small black cat walked inside. It trotted over to the fireplace, batted at one of the logs in the grate, and then turned big amber eyes up at

Aunt Sally and said, "Mere." It was the spittin' image of the cat in Aunt Sally's vision. Alarmed, she said, "Is something wrong with Betty, cat?"

The black cat blinked once and pawed a loose pine knot sitting in the log basket.

Taking that as a yes, Aunt Sally grabbed her shawl and headed out to her son Sam's place. She'd ask Sam to drive her to Blake and Betty's cabin back in the woods. She was climbing the steps to the porch when Blake himself rode up, calling for Sam.

"What's happened?" Aunt Sally cried, staring into her nephew's grim, despairing face as Sam barreled out onto the porch, alarmed by Blake's frantic call.

"Betty's run off with that old spark of hers—Ralph," Blake said grimly. "Her brother Bill's gone after them with his gun. He's furious. I think he may kill Ralph *and* Betty if he meets up with them."

Sam ran for his horse. Aunt Sally watched as the two cousins rode off into the hills to locate the fleeing lovers before the murderous Bill. Somehow, in her heart, she knew it was already too late. She went home and fed the little black cat that— mercifully—lay on a blanket *beside* the hearth, unlike the cat in her vision.

It was Sam who came, many hours later, and sat beside his mother's hearth with the black cat in his lap to tell her the last part of the story. Ralph and Betty had taken to the wild mountain paths in their bid for freedom. They took turns riding Ralph's big white ox with the black spots, switching places every time the person on foot grew weary.

Unbeknownst to the lovers, Betty's brother Bill discovered their trail and climbed the hill in front of them. Finding a fallen

DREAMS AND VISIONS

apple tree, he pruned away the twigs using his white-handled knife to make a perfect blind for his rifle. When Ralph and Betty came up the hill—Ralph riding the black-spotted ox— Bill shot Ralph dead. Betty fled back the way they'd come, and Bill followed her, leaving his white-handled knife by the fallen apple tree. When Blake and Sam arrived, they found Ralph lying dead on the path with his big black-spotted ox lying patiently beside him, waiting for his owner to get up. It was Blake who'd found Bill's white-handled knife and pieced together what had happened. By this time Bill had fled from the mountains— fearing retribution from the authorities—after giving his sister the scolding of her life.

Aunt Sally dabbed at her eyes with her handkerchief, remembering the blood the devil-man had dripped on Betty's hands in her vision. It must have been Ralph's blood, and her niece-in-law would have it on her conscience for the rest of her days.

They buried Ralph on top of the hill. While they were digging the grave, a free-roaming flock of chickens kept pecking around the path and flying into the open grave, much to the annoyance of the grave diggers. So Aunt Sally's dream was fulfilled in every particular.

Betty never strayed from her marriage vows again. And Aunt Sally still has a little black cat with amber eyes that always seems to know exactly what she is thinking. But the devil-man never returned, for which all were thankful.

23

Resurrection

CHARLOTTE

I suppose, looking back, that we could have found a less grisly way to make some money. But at the time jobs were scarce, and a university fellow needed to have some spare change if he wanted to make an impression on the pretty local girls. At least that's what we thought.

It was Charlie who first suggested that we might assist the local medical school in their search for cadavers. He was studying to be a doctor and had heard rumors of the ghost of a girl that supposedly haunted his college. Folks said her body had been stolen and brought to the school for medical research, and her ghost had haunted the school ever since. That's what gave him the idea.

Charlie found out from the friend of a friend that there was money to be had for fresh corpses on the black market. That's when he roped in me and Lester. Three of us could haul around corpses better than just one. Lester and I were a bit dubious at first about Charlie's proposition. I'd been all set to interview for a job at the local pharmacy, and Lester was about to apply for work at the newspaper. But Charlie was persuasive. We could earn more in one night grave robbing than we could earn in a month of honest toil at the pharmacy or the newspaper. Besides, once a person has passed, he or she didn't need the body anymore. Said so right in the Good Book. They were getting a new one, come Judgment Day. *And* we'd be advancing the cause of science. Well, I was in favor of advancing the cause of science. And Lester was always short of money. So we agreed to Charlie's plan.

We chose a moonless night for our first adventure. Lester and Charlie had been scouting all the churches and graveyards in the vicinity, and I'd been watching the newspapers for funeral announcements. Between us, we came up with a couple of good candidates who'd shuffled off the mortal coil in the last few days. As soon as it got dark, we went to work.

"First up, a man named Jonathan Smith," Lester announced as he slid onto the seat of the wagon and picked up the reins.

"Sounds like a pseudonym," said Charlie, sliding in next to him. "I wonder what crime he was hiding."

Soon we were trotting down the road toward a cemetery south of town. We quickly came abreast of a wrought-iron fence that announced the start of the cemetery. Lester cautiously nosed the wagon inside the gates and drove to a corner lot, where the lantern Charlie was holding showed a new headstone and recently disturbed earth. Glancing at the headstone, I read: "Sacred to the memory of my husband Jonathan. His comely young widow yearns to be comforted." Lester laughed when he saw the stone and said, "Here you go, Charlie. You can spark with the Widow Smith!"

I shook my head and handed around the shovels. It was slow, hot work digging up a coffin. We shoveled the dirt onto a canvas tarp laid by the grave, so the nearby grounds remained pristine. We started the digging at the head of the grave clear to the coffin. We covered the lid in sacking to muffle noise, and Lester used a crowbar to pull it free. And there was Mr. Jonathan Smith, resurrected at last, though perhaps not the way he'd been expecting.

The old man was not good to look upon when we pulled him out. Widow Smith had decked him out in his best suit, but his white hair flopped wildly as we lifted him up, and nothing could improve the collapsed, withered look to his face or the greenish tint of his skin in the lantern light. And he smelled awful. Still, money was money. Charlie and I hauled the corpse to the wagon while Lester started filling in the grave. We laid Mr. Smith in back and then helped Lester smooth down the dirt by the headstone. I tossed the canvas on top of Mr. Smith's body to conceal it as we got back into the wagon.

Our second snatch had been buried in a cemetery a little to the east of town. We headed out that way in high spirits. We were going to make a fortune! The only light along the tree-lined avenue came from Charlie's lantern. It made strange flickering shadows on the underside of the branches. You don't realize how noisy the night is—what with the buzz of chirping insects, the rustle of night creatures roaming the bushes, and the calling of night birds—until all that sound ceases abruptly, as it had now. And from somewhere in back of the wagon, a moaning sound began. "*Oooo. Ooooo!*"

The sound started low but grew in volume and rose in pitch until it echoed up and down the shadowy lane and the whole wagon shook with it. My ears hurt, and my teeth buzzed unpleasantly, but that was nothing compared to the shudders of fear shaking my body and the chills crawling all over my skin.

"Cut it out, Charlie. That isn't funny," Lester shouted as the horses nervously swerved first to one side of the road and then to the other, their ears pricked backward in anxiety. His hands were shaking on the reins as we broke out of the tree line into a wide meadow with a cow pond on our left.

"It isn't me!" Charlie retorted over the escalating sound. He clapped shaking hands over his ears and turned to look back over the seat of the wagon. The dirty tarp was shaking as something struggled to rise from underneath. And then a green light came streaming up through the tarp, shooting over our heads like a bright firework, and started spinning in the air. It rapidly formed into the figure of a skinny old man with a withered face and floppy white hair. He flew right at us, fingers outstretched like claws.

Lester shouted in panic. The horses reared and then plunged off the road, racing down the incline and into the shallow pond. The ghost flew after us; his glowing hands pummeled our faces and pulled at our hair. Every blow was ice cold, as if we were being slapped with winter sea water. Behind us, the moaning sound increased until I thought my eardrums would burst. The horses were chest deep in water and trying desperately to swim, but the wagon stuck fast in the muddy bottom and pulled them to a halt.

I leapt out of the wagon into the pond with a great splash. I waded as fast as I could through muddy water and bulrushes, chased by the irate ghost. As soon as I hit dry land, I ran for my life. The glowing man whirled back toward the wagon and pummeled the escaping Charlie and Lester around the ears as they followed me up the slope and down the road. I risked a quick look behind me and saw the moaning corpse of Jonathan

Smith rolling in the wagon bed, all tangled up in the tarp. The glowing ghost swooped and tried to free his corpse from the tarp, but his spirit hands were unable to grip it. The horses rolled their eyes in panic but were stuck fast and unable to flee from the frightening vision. I kept running.

Fatigue forced us to a halt, and we lay panting in the center of the dark avenue. We knew we had to go back. We couldn't leave the wagon and the horses in the pond. "And," I said aloud, "we have to rebury the body."

Charlie groaned but didn't argue with me. None of us wanted to mess with moaning corpses or savage ghosts for the rest of our lives.

We waited until the shrieks of outrage had ceased before we crept back along the avenue and crouched at the edge of the tree line, looking for the ghost. All was silent in the meadow, and the horses were shifting restlessly in the water as they tried in vain to free themselves from the harness. The body in the wagon bed had ceased moaning and lay still.

Hastily, we pushed and pulled at the wagon until it came unstuck from the pond mud, and we guided the trembling horses out of the pond and back up the hill. Then Lester drove at top speed back to the cemetery, and we re-interred Jonathan Smith next to the stone put up by his hopeful widow. It was full daylight before we got to Lester's house, and we still had to wash the mud off the wagon before we called it quits for the night.

"Shall we go again tomorrow?" Charlie asked half-heartedly when the last bit of mud was removed. Lester and I glared at him. "Or maybe not," he mumbled, backing away hastily. "I'll see you both later." He hastened out of the barn and ran out of

RESURRECTION

the yard, a rumpled figure in water-stained trousers and weedy boots.

"There's got to be a better way to earn money," I said to Lester as I tossed a dirty rag into the rain barrel.

"I'm going to work for the newspaper," Lester said flatly. "And I refuse to cover the obits."

He walked out of the barn without looking back. I watched him go ruefully and then headed home myself. If I hurried, I could get cleaned up and still make that job interview at the pharmacy. Even if I didn't get the position, I was sure of one thing: My body-snatching days were over! I'd find some other way of earning cash.

24

The White Deer

There is a legend told of a time long ago when a group of English colonists bravely left their homes to travel to a new world. They settled on the island of Roanoke, and while they were there, a small girl-child was born to the daughter of the new governor. The baby was named Virginia in honor of Elizabeth I, the Virgin Queen.

Concerned for the well-being of his small colony, the governor traveled back to his homeland for supplies—and found himself trapped there by a war between England and Spain. For three years he was kept from his beloved daughter, his new grandchild, and the good people who had settled in his colony. Finally, he boarded a ship and sailed for the New World and for the City of Raleigh he'd left behind.

The governor arrived on Roanoke Island on August 18, 1590—his granddaughter's third birthday—and found it empty. No welcoming daughter and son-in-law. No toddling grandbaby. No settlers. The City of Raleigh was deserted, plundered, and surrounded by a palisade of great trees, as if it were a fort. On one of the palisades, he found the single word *croatoan* carved into the surface, and the letters *cro* carved into a nearby tree.

Hoping this meant that the colony (and his family) had gone to stay with his friend Chief Manteo on present-day Hatteras Island, the governor was preparing to follow them when a great hurricane arose, damaging his ships and forcing him to return to England. He was never able to fund another trip to America and died without knowing what had happened to his family. Indeed, no one ever found out what happened to the Lost Colony. It remains a mystery to this day.

But the whispers of American legend tell a further story about the lost colonists. Not the story of a people slaughtered or a people lost. It is a story of a family displaced from their home by the hostility of island natives, a story of a family taken in by a neighboring tribe on the far side of the island and welcomed with open arms. And it is the story of a little baby girl with bright blue eyes and long flowing hair who was beloved by all who met her and much missed by her grieving grandfather, who died alone in England.

Virginia Dare grew wise in the ways of the forest, strong in her understanding of man and beast. And with each year she grew more comely and desirable until all the eligible warriors in the tribe were in love with her. The young chief Okisko was the bravest and the most handsome of the warriors, and his suit found favor with the lovely Virginia Dare, and with her doting parents. But the medicine man Chico was not pleased by the match. He desired the lovely girl for himself and would not allow her to go to another. A wizard coached in the dark arts, he called on the spirits and caused a spell to fall upon Virginia Dare, transforming her into a white deer as she walked alone near the sound one summer evening. With a bleat of fear and confusion, the white deer fled into the trees and bracken, lost to the sight of the cunning sorcerer.

The Dare family was alarmed when their daughter did not return from her stroll that evening. Everyone in the tribe was alerted; settlers and tribesmen alike searched the island for the beloved girl. But she had vanished and was presumed drowned in the sea. None of the people looking for the girl associated her disappearance with the appearance of a white deer that could sometimes be seen walking near the sound at dusk.

Only Okisko believed that she might still be alive. The grieving suitor spent many days in prayer and fasting, seeking knowledge of the lovely Virginia from the spirit world. On the afternoon of the third day, a brown pelican came to him on the winds of the sea and told him that Virginia had been transformed into a white deer by the black wizard Chico. The only way to free her was to pierce her heart with an arrow tipped by an oyster shell. Rejoicing in this good news, Okisko thanked the proud spirit of the brown pelican and immediately found an oyster shell, which he made into the head of an arrow.

Unbeknownst to Okisko, the evil Chico had revealed to one of the girl's rejected suitors—Wanchese—that the white deer grazing along the sound was none other than the missing Virginia Dare. Chico hoped that the jealous warrior would kill the doe, thus completing his revenge against the Englishwoman.

Wanchese hated the English who had settled among his people. Most especially did he hate Virginia Dare, who had favored Okisko's suit over his own. He had traveled to England with the first explorers and there had learned of a substance called silver that would kill the creatures created by black magic.

167

Having some coins in his possession from that long-ago trip, he melted the metal in a hot fire and made an arrowhead of pure silver. As dusk fell over the island, Wanchese went hunting for the white deer down by the sound.

On the seaside of the island, the brown pelican flew urgently across the waves toward Okisko, who was affixing the oyster-shell tip to his arrow. "Hurry," the brown pelican called to him. "You must hurry. Another seeks for the white deer and would take her life!"

Okisko gasped in horror and ran across the island as fast as his strong body would carry him toward the place where the white deer had been seen walking beside the sound. As he reached the abandoned place where the City of Raleigh once stood, he saw the white deer walking down on the sandy shore. He took aim at once, the gleaming oyster-shell at the tip of his arrow, and shot the white deer in the heart. At the same moment, a silver-tipped arrow flew through the air from the far side of the clearing, and it too pierced the heart of the white deer.

The white deer gave a cry like that of a woman in pain. Its form shimmered, glowing so brightly that it blinded the eyes of the two warriors who had shot her. Then the light died away, and they saw, lying on the ground where the white deer had stood, the dying figure of beautiful Virginia Dare.

Okisko gave a wail of anguish and ran to his beloved's side. Behind him Wanchese laughed—an evil sound—and disappeared into the bracken—never to be seen again. Virginia Dare died in her beloved's arms and was buried in the old fort where her people had first settled. Okisko went on to become a great chief among his people, but he never married. His people

THE WHITE DEER

whispered that the source of his success came from his spirit guide—a white deer who would appear sometimes to him at dusk down by the shores of the sound.

To this day, whenever a white deer appears along the shores of the Outer Banks, it is said that the spirit of Virginia Dare has returned to watch over the land that she once loved.

25

The Legend of Tsali

GREAT SMOKY MOUNTAINS NATIONAL PARK

I watch over these high hills through the mist and the wind, the heat and the snow. I walk the deer paths over Clingman's Dome and wander the roadways and streams, drifting across the deep valleys at will. I guard my people and my land, as I have always done. As I always will. Most people who visit here never see me, and I am content that it be so. But to a chosen few who have the right eye and the right spirit, I appear with the dawn and the dusk, a Cherokee warrior whose spirit has never left his mountain home. As the sun sets over this high valley, I sit on an old stump at my favorite lookout and remember . . .

I remember that my people were forced to leave. In the end we had no choice. We had done everything the white men asked of us, adopting many of their ways, building roads and schools and churches. We even developed a system of representational government, and a brilliant Cherokee linguist named Sequoyah developed the written Cherokee alphabet—the Talking Leaves— without having any previous knowledge of a written script.

We were a people of peace. Many of us were farmers and cattle ranchers. But white settlers were rapidly filling the southern states, and the Cherokee lands—which extended from

Georgia to the Ohio River—were at the heart of the crossroads of commerce. This flood of settlers increased tensions between us and our white brothers. And then gold was found on Cherokee land. At that moment, the fate of our nation was sealed. In 1830 the Congress of the United States passed the Indian Removal Act, declaring that my people and many other tribes living in the South were to be sent away from the bones of our ancestors to live in Oklahoma Territory.

So we fought back. Not with spears and bows as we might once have fought. This time we used the laws of state and nation, up to the highest courts. And we won a reprieve, for the Supreme Court of the land said we were an independent nation and could not be removed unless a treaty was signed between ourselves and the U.S. government.

But the public tide was against us, even when the courts ruled in our favor. And soon some of the Cherokee were swayed to the side of removal, wearied by the long, hard battle against the U.S. government. And so they sold our birthright for $5 million and signed the Treaty of New Echota, giving President Andrew Jackson the legal document he needed to remove us from our lands.

Still, our advocates—like the statesman Davy Crockett—fought on our behalf. But the ratification of the treaty passed the Senate by one vote, and just like that, we lost our land. In May 1838 U.S. General Winfield Scott and his army invaded the Cherokee Nation, slashing and burning, seizing cattle, and thrusting families from their homes and into makeshift forts with minimal facilities and little food.

I was living in the Smoky Mountains in a small cabin with my wife and sons while the turmoil of politics raged in

Washington, D.C. I hunted and farmed the land and was far more concerned with the weather and my crops than with the goings-on of people who lived far away from my hills— that is, until my brother-in-law came for a visit to our cabin in May 1838 to tell us about the companies of soldiers who were searching the valleys of our home and herding thousands of Cherokee people into stockades in preparation for a great march to the west. It seemed fantastical to me at the time. How could such a thing be? But my brother-in-law was an honest man, and it must be so.

I was troubled as I returned to my fields to work. How would this affect my family? Would we be forced from our home in the hills of our ancestors? As I worked, sweat pouring down my back and legs, I saw in a flash a picture of my people living and working, laughing and crying and playing in these mountains many years into the future. They would be born here, wed here, die here, and would carry on the traditions and wisdom passed to us from our ancestors. I paused, stunned by this dream that had come to my mind. Was it possible? Could we resist this removal and win?

I made my way home when the work was done, still pondering my dream of the future. And shortly I found myself and my family confronted by white soldiers, who came to my cabin and ordered us to join the other Cherokee in the stockade at Bushnell. We were given little time to prepare for the journey and could take with us only the belongings we could carry.

All of us—myself, my wife, my sons, and my brother-in-law—left home under the guard of the soldiers. Outwardly, I was calm, and my stillness kept my sons calm. Inwardly, I was furious. How dare they force us off our land? I had signed no treaty. I had not even known there was a treaty until my brother-in-law had arrived. In front of me, my dear wife stumbled in fatigue, and one of the soldiers prodded her cruelly with his bayonet. I clenched my fists in rage and then spoke softly to my kinsmen in Cherokee, which the soldiers did not appear to understand. "When we reach the turn in the trail," I said to my sons, "I will trip and fall and complain of my ankle. When the soldiers stop, leap upon them and take their guns. Then we'll escape into the hills."

At the appropriate moment, I fell down on the path, miming an injury, and my sons leapt upon their captors with the help of my brother-in-law. In the short fracas that followed, a rifle went off, and one of the soldiers fell dead onto the forest floor. We fled then, knowing that the fury of the white men would follow us.

I led us up into the mountains to a concealed cave I knew of under the peak known as Clingman's Dome, knowing the white man's troops would be at a disadvantage in such a place, should they be able to track us this far. By the time we settled ourselves for the night, I knew that I would fight to the death rather than allow my family to become prisoners of the U.S. Army.

We lived as fugitives through the long summer that followed, foraging as best we could and avoiding the white soldiers who hunted us. Around us, the destruction continued, until the last band of Cherokee under the guardianship of U.S. soldiers left in the autumn for the west. It was at this time that Will Thomas, a white trader who had been adopted by a Cherokee chief, came to our cave on Clingman's Dome. He told us about the other Cherokee—numbering about a thousand—who had taken refuge in the mountains. Then he relayed a message from the U.S. General Scott, whose soldier had died in the fracas with my family: "If Tsali and his kin will come in and give up, I won't hunt down the others. If Tsali will voluntarily pay the penalty, I will intercede with the government to grant the fugitives permission to remain. But if Tsali refuses, I'll turn my soldiers loose to hunt every one of them."

We sat in silence in the cave, thinking about the general's words. Will Thomas looked into the fire, avoiding our eyes. In my mind I saw again that flash of vision I had in the field, the day I lost my farm: my people living and working, laughing and loving and dying in these mountains as they carried on the traditions and wisdom passed to us from our ancestors. I had shared this vision with my family, and as I looked from one face to another, I saw the same determination in each one. If our deaths could bring about such a future, how could we say no?

And so we turned ourselves in. I embraced my wife and wiped the tears from her eyes. Then we left our hiding place. We were met by a band of the Oconaluftee Cherokee who lived in Quallatown, those for whom our sacrifice would be made, and they brought us to the stockade. The trial was swiftly over. My son, my brother-in-law, and I were sentenced to die, but my wife and youngest son were spared. We were taken to the field next to the stockade and were stood against three trees. The colonel in charge asked us for our final words, and I said, "If I must be killed, I would like to be shot by my own people." I confess, I was surprised when they acceded to my request. Three Cherokee men were selected to be our executioners, and I saw in their faces that they understood the sacrifice we were making on behalf of our people. I glanced at my brother-in-law and at my brave son, who had lived so gallantly all his short life.

THE LEGEND OF TSALI

He gave me a nod, and we both looked into the barrels of the guns pointed at us, waving aside the offer of blindfolds. Then shots rang out in the valley, and our bodies fell to the earth, to be buried beside the stockade.

At that moment my spirit could have gone to be with my ancestors. My son and my brother-in-law certainly followed the sacred path before them. But I lingered behind in these mountains where I had lived and died. I wanted to watch over my wife and younger son. And I wanted to see whether our sacrifice made any difference for our people and whether the white man would keep his word.

And he did. The white man ruled that the Quallatown Cherokee who lived outside the official boundaries of the Cherokee Nation were not required by law to emigrate, and that those Cherokee still hiding in the mountains might join with them and live freely. And so the federal troops left our homeland . . .

And so I have remained, from that day to this, as a silent watcher over my people. We have grown in number through the years. Ten thousand Cherokee now live in the center of our ancient homeland. I guard their sleep and watch over their dreams as they live and work, laugh and love and die in these mountains and carry on the traditions and wisdom passed to us from our ancestors.

I stand, now and forever, at the soul and center of this land. My people call me Tsali.

26

Mercy

SMITHFIELD

The lieutenant had heard, of course, about the Union marauders following in the wake of General William Tecumseh Sherman, plundering houses, killing families, destroying what they did not steal. He had considered it despicable behavior and had spoken out against it, in the abstract. But the reality was not driven home to him until he walked into the ruins of his house in Smithfield and found both of his beloved parents dead at the hands of the most ruthless band of Union marauders that had ever pillaged the South.

As he buried his father—Confederate Colonel John Saunders—and his lovely, gentle mother in the family graveyard under a big tree, the lieutenant swore that he would exact vengeance against the men who had murdered them. And he knew exactly who they were. The David Fanning gang was fifty men strong, and they had been ransacking the countryside for months. Grimly, he went back to his commanding officer and requested a troop of men to help him track down the marauders. Sympathetic to his cause, the general granted his request.

For the next several weeks, the lieutenant and his men traveled through the countryside in search of the renegades.

But every lead petered out, every hint came to nothing. The lieutenant had never felt so frustrated in his life. The vision of his sweet mother's dead face was ever before his eyes, and the gruff voice of his father haunted his dreams at night. Surely, if there was a good God in heaven, justice must be done for these blameless, beloved folk!

There came a rustle from outside his door, and a soldier entered with an air of barely suppressed excitement. "They've been spotted, sir," he blurted out after the minimum of courtesies. "The marauders appear to have set up camp on an island in Hannah's Creek Swamp."

The lieutenant went very still as he absorbed the news. Hannah's Creek Swamp. He knew the place. It was remote, and the island at its center was a good place to hide. A flame of excitement swelled in his chest. Yes. This was it. He could feel it.

The young soldier eyed his commanding officer with concern. The lieutenant had not said a word since he made his report. Understanding the situation a little better, the older officer on duty at the door laid a hand on the lad's arm and gestured him quietly away. Then he went in to the lieutenant and asked for orders. The lieutenant looked up at last with fire in his eyes and ordered an immediate march on the swamp.

As they broke camp, the lieutenant realized that disguises would be necessary in order for them to safely reach the island without tipping off the marauders. When they reached Smithfield, they borrowed civilian clothing from the locals, who were happy to help the lieutenant sent to rescue them from David Fanning's band of killers.

Commandeering rowboats, the lieutenant set out across the swamp with his men. He stood in the lead boat and answered the hails from the island. "Union soldiers," he called when asked to identify himself. "We were forced out of the last county and heard there were Union soldiers near Smithfield. We are hoping to join your troop."

The leader of the marauders stepped to the edge of the shore and stared out at the disguised lieutenant. The eyes of the two men met, and the lieutenant's body stiffened as he realized he was looking at David Fanning, the man who had ordered the deaths of his parents. It took a great effort to keep his face still and calm.

"What unit?" Fanning called across the water.

"Sherman's XIV corps," the lieutenant called back with a grim smile, remembering how fiercely the Yankees in that corps had fought in the Battle of Bentonville.

Smiles broke out on the faces of the marauders, and they shouted welcomes to the men bearing down on them in boats. The lieutenant stepped ashore and came face-to-face with David Fanning.

"What's your name, brother?" Fanning asked jovially, holding out his hand.

"I am called John Saunders," the lieutenant said softly, refusing to take the outstretched hand. "Named for my father."

All around him, the Confederate soldiers' guns came up. The marauders were quickly surrounded and subdued. The color drained from Fanning's face as he recognized the name of Saunders.

"Search them," Saunders said grimly. He wanted no mistakes made in this raid. The men were searched, and Confederate plunder was found aplenty. And around the neck of Fanning himself was a crucifix of gold that the lieutenant had last seen adorning the neck of his beloved mother.

Enraged, he yanked the necklace from Fanning's neck and forced him to kneel with a gun to the back of his head. "You— all of you—are hereby found guilty of theft, marauding, and murder," the lieutenant said without emotion. Nodding to his sergeant, he said, "Hang them from the neck until they are dead."

The Confederate soldiers were quick to obey. Fanning gasped a protest, but a nudge from the gun at the back of his skull silenced him. Ropes were noosed around the necks of the marauders—fifty strong—and they were hauled up into the gnarled trees of the island in the swamp and hanged until they were dead.

Fanning, forced to kneel on the ground and watch his men die, alternated between angry curses and pleas for mercy. He was ignored.

When the last marauder was dead, Saunders ordered his men to the boats. They left the bodies of the Union soldiers hanging from the trees and dragged Fanning, tied hand and foot, into the lead boat. Then they force-marched the leader of the marauders back to Smithfield and down a familiar lane to an old family graveyard near the Saunderses' pillaged home.

When he saw the two brand-new gleaming white stones in the graveyard, Fanning dug in his heels and refused to walk a step farther. "Mercy," he gasped. "Mercy, I beg you." Then he looked into the lieutenant's eyes.

"Where was the mercy you showed when you stole this?" the lieutenant asked, holding up the gold crucifix. "The same mercy meted out by you is the mercy I offer you now."

He nodded to his sergeant. "Hang him."

The sergeant nodded and looped a rope around David Fanning's neck. The marauder was hanged until he was dead

MERCY

from the tree growing above the graves of the elder Saunderses, his feet dangling over the gleaming white headstones.

The lieutenant stooped before his mother's grave and laid the crucifix tenderly on the stone. Justice was served. But somehow, it didn't make him feel any better. With his whole soul, he longed to see his mother one last time. To see her smile. To make her laugh.

He turned away and walked out of the graveyard as his men cut the dead Fanning down from the tree. Justice. Mercy. Duty. Revenge. The lieutenant was sick of it all. He just wanted to go home.

For years after the Southern surrender in Yorktown, rumors circulated about the Hannah's Creek ghosts. Folks wandering through the swamp or boating on the small lake claimed they could hear pleas for mercy and see ghostly bodies hanging from the gnarled trees. Such was its reputation that people started avoiding the place, until it was completely reclaimed by the wilderness and the island was swallowed up by the swamp. But they say if you roam near Hannah's Creek at night, you can still hear David Fanning pleading for mercy as his men are strung up on ghostly, gnarled trees that no longer exist.

27

Jubilee

VANDEMERE

Boom! Boom! Boooom!

My twelve-year-old daughter, Hannah, and I were sitting down to a belated afternoon lunch when we were startled by a massive thunderclap of sound like the booming of cannon.

Boooom!

My seven-year-old son, Jason, who had eaten earlier, shot into the kitchen with a yell of sheer delight: "Jubilee! Jubilee!"

He grabbed my hand and tried to pull me out of my chair, shouting, "Come on, Mom!"

Hannah whooped and jumped out of her chair, her glass of milk tumbling to the floor behind her. "I'll get the tongs and the shovels," Hannah yelled, blonde hair wild about her face as she pounded out of the kitchen, heading for the back hall closet.

My husband, Carl, flew into the kitchen next. "Nets! Marie, where are the nets?"

"In the garage where they always are," I said, a calm center in the midst of chaos. I calmly took another sip of coffee as I shooed Jason and Carl toward the garage.

Boom! Boom!

Like our neighbors to the south, we Vandemere folk sometimes hear the loud reporting of the "Seneca Guns." The sound is a mystery. As sharp and echoing as cannon fire, it vibrates up and down the coast, startling everyone who hears it. Doors and windows tremble and reverberate in sympathy when it starts, adding to the racket. No one can trace its source or discover why it happens. It has baffled scientists for years, but we locals have grown accustomed to it over the decades and simply call it the Seneca Guns.

In Vandemere the sound of the Seneca Guns triggers a second natural phenomenon: the Jubilee. Nobody really knows why the Jubilee comes with the sound of the Seneca Guns. But we are sure glad it does. A Jubilee occurs when many species of crab and shrimp, as well as flounder, eels, and other fish, leave deeper waters and congregate—in large numbers and very high density—in the shallow waters by the shore. First, minnows and small fish race toward the shore as if they were trying to beach themselves. They are rapidly followed by larger fish, crabs, and sometimes even scallops. For about an hour, the shallow waters teem with sea creatures of all kinds while the Seneca Guns boom. But the harvest is so plentiful that we are still eating from it a month later.

Scientists say that a Jubilee occurs when deeper parts of the sound undergo a rapid depletion of oxygen, which drives fish to the surface seeking oxygenated water. But that doesn't explain why such low levels of oxygen start whenever the Seneca Guns sound, or stop when the Seneca Guns stop.

Boom! Boom! Boooom!

In the back bedroom my two-year-old son, Chris, started wailing softly, wakened from his nap by all the noise and confusion. Outside I could hear the neighbors calling to one another as they grabbed baskets, buckets, shovels, tongs, whatever they could get their hands on to help with the harvest. Everyone in town knew what it meant when the Seneca Guns started booming in Vandemere.

"Crab walk!" I heard someone yell in the road out front.

"Time of Jubilee!" came the answer from my neighbor across the street.

Boom went the Seneca Guns up and down the coast. The noise was so loud that it rattled the windows in the nursery. Little Chris held his arms up to me as I reached his bed. I swept him up, feeling a lump in my throat. The last time the Seneca Guns had boomed along this coast, my mother was still alive. She had watched little Chris while the rest of us ran down to the beach for the harvest. But Mom was dead now—passed in her sleep from a silent heart attack. I didn't relish taking my two-year-old into the chaos on the beach, but I couldn't leave him behind. And Hannah was old enough to help watch him while we harvested shrimp and crabs and fish from the teeming waters.

It took five minutes to get everything assembled. Pulling Chris in a small wagon filled with a cooler and several baskets, I followed my family out into the bustling streets, joining the dancing, singing, exclaiming crowd headed to the shore.

Boom! Boom! Boooom!

By the time we arrived, the shallows were boiling with fish. Crabs scuttled from the shallows to the shore, and then back into the shallows. I could see scallops jetting back and forth like small torpedoes under the lapping waves.

Jason and Hannah raced into the water in their cutoffs and old sneakers and started pitching fish into a basket they had jammed in the doughnut hole of an automobile inner tube. Carl was after crabs—his favorite—netting them carefully and tossing them into a cooler. People thronged the beach, enthusiastically wading into the water with crab nets and tongs and shovels. Children raced around in circles and splashed themselves silly, parents shouted instructions, and old fishermen calmly netted the largest fish. Chaos surrounded us, and the noise level made my ears ring, but it was great fun just the same!

Boom! Boooom!

In the shallows, submerged in a few inches of water, crabs were stacked up in rows as dense as cars in a parking lot. There were a lot of fish species too: small fish and flounder struggling along at the edge where tiny waves lapped the shore, their upper gill covers rising into the air in a desperate search for oxygen.

Little Chris wiggled and wiggled in my arms, wanting to wade into the water with his brother and sister. Hannah, seeing my dilemma, shouted, "It's okay, Mom. I'll watch him. You go help Dad."

She shoved aside a couple of gasping flounder and took him from my arms. I smiled in relief. Chris was getting heavy now that he was two. I was really thankful for that babysitting class Hannah took last year. It was worth every blessed penny we paid.

I grabbed for one of the shovels and scooped it under a flounder, heaving it into the cooler with Carl's crabs. Flounder was *my* favorite meal. And I wanted to scoop up some of those scallops before my next-door neighbor cornered the market.

Boom! Boom! Boooom! The Seneca Guns were still vibrating up and down the coastline, eclipsing even the noise of the crowd.

Suddenly, Hannah was beside me, dripping wet and pale with fright. "Mom! Mom! I can't find Chris!"

I dropped my shovel into the water, and it disappeared under the silvery streaks of thousands of minnows. "What do you mean you can't find Chris!" I shouted, panic ripping through me, my eyes already scanning the crowded shoreline.

Hannah was fighting back tears. "He was holding my hand, and we were wading at the edge of the water when I tripped over a stone and fell into the water right on top of a huge crab. I must have dropped Chris's hand when I fell, because I couldn't find him anywhere when I got back on my feet!"

"You go tell your father and brother. I'll start searching," I gasped through a tight throat. "Where were you when you fell?"

Hannah pointed to the spot and then ran down the beach toward Carl. I raced in the opposite direction, toward the spot where my baby had disappeared, bumping into neighbors, friends, and children running back and forth to baskets and buckets and coolers on the beach, their nets full of flopping fish and scuttling crabs. I asked everyone about Chris. No one had seen him. Many people broke off their harvesting to help me search the shallows. The body of a small boy could easily be hidden under the teeming fish in the water. My heart clenched at the morbid thought, and I shook it off. Chris was fine. He had to be!

Boom! Boooom! The Seneca Guns roared their mysterious message up and down the beach.

And then I saw a familiar little figure in tiny khaki shorts and a white T-shirt. He was walking up the beach toward me, holding the hand of an elderly woman in a flower-print dress.

JUBILEE

I froze in shock, recognizing the woman at once. My heart thudded painfully against my ribs, and I broke into a cold sweat, unable to take my eyes off the woman's laughing face. It was my dead mother!

Chris was chuckling and pointing at the fish squirming their way out of the water. My mother was saying the name of each kind of fish he pointed to. Neither of them saw me. Then Chris looked past a couple of kids hauling a large flounder out of the shallows by its gills and saw me.

"Mommy," he shouted. Dropping my mother's hand, he ran to me and flung his arms around my legs. My knees gave way, and I fell onto the hard, wet sand, clutching him close while tears poured down my cheeks. All the time, I stared up at my mother, who was wearing her favorite flower-print dress that we'd buried her in. She smiled at me lovingly, just as she had in life. And then she was gone, just like that.

A moment later I felt Carl's arms close around me. He was shaking with relief. Then Hannah and Jason piled on top of us, nearly toppling me to the ground. A crab scuttled past us, heading up the beach as fast as it could. I hardly noticed.

Boooom! The sound was fainter now, fading away. And the fish were not so plentiful in the shallows. The scallops had already jetted away, and the fish were following. We helped each other up, clinging together gratefully. Hannah was frantic with sorrow, apologizing again and again. Finally, Carl picked her up like he had when she was a little girl. "You didn't mean to fall," he said, wiping away her tears. "Chris could have gotten away from any of us in this crowd. It's all right now."

"Hannah cry," Chris observed with concern.

Jubilee

"Hannah will be okay in a minute," I told him. Jason trotted along beside us, wordless with relief. Then he spotted our abandoned baskets and raced forward to claim them before they went home with another family. Carl put Hannah down and shooed her after Jason. I clung tightly to Chris as my husband and children gathered up our tools and the baskets and cooler full of crabs, scallops, and other bounty from the sea. It was time to go home.

I packed Chris in among the filled baskets and pushed him home in the wagon. All the time I thought about what I had seen on the beach. My mother—my dead mother—had rescued her grandson when he became lost in the crowd. It seemed impossible. But that was what I'd seen.

Mom had looked younger than she had when I last saw her. And she looked happy, for which I was thankful. I bent toward my young son and whispered, "Who did you see at the beach, Chris?" Chris, his fingers tightly curled around the handle of the cooler, looked up with a grin. "Grammy," he said. "I see Grammy!"

My heart contracted inside me, with the pain of my mother's loss combined with the joy of seeing her one more time. The lump in my throat was so huge that I couldn't speak. I just brushed my baby's hair from his forehead and looked across the wagon at Carl. I'd tell him about Mom when we got home, I decided. Right now, I was too filled up with joy and relief to say a word. I just smiled at my family, thanking God for a beautiful summer day and a successful Jubilee.

28

Raven Mockers

CHEROKEE

He woke out of a sound sleep, trembling from head to toe, unsure what had caused him to wake. The house was silent except for the soft breathing of his wife. And outside the walls, a strange hush lay over the world. Save for the soft whisper of the wind, there were no sounds at all. He kept waiting for the stealthy rustle of a passing fox, the grunt of a bear, the soft whisper of an owl's wings. But there was nothing.

Then he heard the sharp, unmistakable cry of a diving raven. He knew then what had awakened him. The Raven Mockers were gathering. Which meant that someone in the village was dying. He broke into a cold sweat, rising swiftly and fumbling into his clothes. His wife rolled over without waking as he grabbed for his bow and headed out the door. Who was sick? Who was dying? No one had reported an illness, though he had noticed old Galilani, a Beloved Woman of the tribe, had a bad cough when he last saw her. Beloved Woman was a prestigious title given to extraordinary women by the Cherokee clans. Galilani headed the Council of Women, held a voting seat in the Council of Chiefs, and had responsibility over prisoners. She was an important person in their village. Too important to lose to the Raven Mockers.

He paused on his doorstep, trying to orient himself. Then he saw the fiery shapes floating overhead, arms outstretched like wings and sparks trailing behind them. Yes, they were headed east, toward the house where old Galilani lived with her widowed daughter. He ran then, as fast as he had ever run. The witches would torment their victim, frightening her, throwing her to the floor, and pummeling her until she died. Then they would remove the heart of their victim and eat it, adding all the hours and days she might have survived to their own lives. And no one in the house would know about it, for the Raven Mockers could make themselves invisible.

He was one of the few medicine men who could see the Raven Mockers in their invisible form, and so he was always called to attend the sick and dying to help keep the witches away. Not knowing what he would find when he reached the house, he pulled one of the special arrows he saved for such witches from his quiver so that it would be ready.

Yes, there was a light on. He ran to the door, knocking and entering at the same time. It was a small, one-room cabin, and the widowed daughter was bent over a small bed where her mother lay. She was surrounded by withered creatures outlined in fire, their gnarled hands poking and prodding the still figure on the bed. The daughter turned when she heard someone enter the room. Her eyes widened when she saw him in the doorway with an arrow already nocked. But she understood at once what it meant.

"Drop," he told her, his voice tight but calm. She fell to the floor, and he shot his magic arrow straight at the closest Raven Mocker. It screamed and writhed in agony as the arrow pierced its heart. Then it vanished in a cloud of sparks, and he knew its foul spirit had returned to its body far away. The other Raven Mockers wailed when they saw the medicine man in their midst. Generally, they hid from such holy men. The evil spells that dominated the life of a Raven Mocker dictated that for the witch to be effective, he or she must live in disguise. If a Raven Mocker was recognized in its human guise, the spells would turn against it, and he or she would die within a week. And holy men, such as the medicine man, were notoriously good at spotting a Raven Mocker in human form once they have seen its spirit.

Only one witch remained calm as the medicine man rapidly nocked a second arrow. Staying focused, it slapped the old woman so hard on the face that her neck snapped, and she fell back dead. The medicine man's second arrow pierced the heart of the killer, but the witch beside it pulled out a flaming knife and slipped it between the old woman's ribs. His third arrow killed the witch before it could cut out the Beloved Woman's heart, and his fourth arrow eliminated another. Each disappeared in a shower of sparks.

The widowed daughter sprawled on the floor, staring from the grim medicine man to the bed where her dead mother lay. She could see the magic arrows flying through the air and then vanishing, but nothing more. The assembled Raven Mockers remained invisible to her eyes.

Overwhelmed by the ferocity of the medicine man's attack, the remaining Raven Mockers dispersed, trailing their fiery way straight through the walls and ceilings of the cabin. The medicine man gasped with relief as the last of them disappeared, and then he strode forward to offer the daughter a hand up. Reading in his face that the danger was over, she fled to the bed and fell weeping upon her dead mother.

"It happened so quickly," she told the medicine man. "She just had a bad cough until this evening. She woke up gasping for breath about an hour ago, and I was so busy attending her that I had no time to send for you."

"Pneumonia," he said, quietly closing the old woman's eyes. "At least the Raven Mockers did not take her heart."

They would have to watch over the body now until burial, or the Raven Mockers would return. Once the old woman was buried, her heart was safe. He sent the widowed daughter to call for her brother and his spouse to join their vigil. At dawn he sent a message to his wife so that she would not be frightened by his sudden absence. Then he arranged a quick burial for Galilani, since she had almost been taken by Raven Mockers.

The whole village turned out to bid farewell to the Beloved Woman, who had been a favorite of many. The medicine man stood silent watch over the proceedings and thought about the Raven Mockers he had marked with his arrows. The witches had come swiftly to torture their victim when she fell ill. So they could not live far away. He was shaken by the number of them. He had counted six witches by the old woman's bedside, and of those he had marked four with his arrows. Now, watching the grief of the family at the unexpected passing of their mother, he felt determination rise within him. No more would these evil witches harm his people or shorten their lives. He was going raven hunting.

He was confident he could find the four he had shot with his magic arrows. He would have to trust that the spirits would guide him to the other two.

The medicine man consulted briefly with the council elders after the burial. His strong medicine was known to them, and they approved of his plan to rid the tribe of the local witches. With their blessing he set off on his self-appointed task.

First, he spent two days in the sweat lodge, praying and seeking wisdom for his hunt. Then he set out with his magic arrows, his knife, and a rifle for more ordinary hunting. He circled the village once, twice, seeking signs of the Raven Mockers' recent passage through the air. The spirit sparks that followed them surely must have injured more than one tree. Praying for the keen eyesight of the eagle and the agility of the squirrel, he climbed several likely-looking tall trees. On the third one he found the small char marks for which he searched.

Dropping back to the ground, he followed the overgrown trail beneath it for more than an hour, until he found a small cabin tucked away into a hollow in the mountain. A middle-aged man was chopping wood behind the cabin, and a woman was doing laundry by the stream bed that passed through one corner of the hollow. It was a perfectly ordinary scene. But the medicine man could see more. His spirit sight perceived the red glow coming through the man's rough shirt in the region of his heart. At the medicine man's side, the magic arrows glowed in response. Then the woman turned, and he saw a similar red glow at her shoulder. Aha! The spirits were with him. He had found two Raven Mockers less than an hour from the village. Nocking an arrow, he stepped into the clearing.

The man and woman looked up at his approach. They recognized him at once, and fear twisted their faces. For a moment all the extra time they had stolen from their victims sat upon their countenances, turning them withered and old and twisted. Then they fled the clearing while he rained arrows after them. He didn't bother to kill them. He'd seen the truth in their faces and knew the witches were doomed. He could hear the woman weeping as she fled.

It took the medicine man two more days to find the next Raven Mocker. He was nearing a local village when he heard the familiar raven screech and heard the strong wind that accompanied it. Sparks were shooting through the roof of a local house.

"Raven Mocker," he shouted to a few men walking the path near him. He was well known in this village for his gift of medicine sight, and the men instantly followed him toward the house. The local holy man was already there, glaring defiantly around the room with sacred objects held ready in his hands. He did not have the same gift of sight as the medicine man, but his holy senses knew that danger was near. He nodded welcome to the men in the doorway as he stood guard over the little child in the cradle that was the Raven Mocker's object.

The medicine man nocked his magic arrows, watching from the doorway. Then he let fly, and the magic arrow shot straight through the throat of the Raven Mocker lurking near the hearth. It disappeared in a shower of sparks. Instantly he followed the sparks, seeing the witch's spirit rise above the treetops as it fled back to its body. A mile down the path, the medicine man found a wrinkled old man crouched over a tiny fire within a circle of evergreens. He sat so still that he might have been dead, but the medicine man knew better. He saw the flaming spirit of the Raven Mocker descending through the sky toward the body. But he had found it first. He sent a magic arrow through the heart of the old man. As the dead body tumbled to the ground, the witch's spirit burst into flames in midair and disappeared.

The medicine man returned in triumph to the village with the body of the witch, and they buried him deep beneath a stone. There was great rejoicing in the village, for the witch had been menacing and dominating them for many years, and no one had been able to touch him until that day. The village elders begged him to stay and eat with them, but the medicine man had three more Raven Mockers to track and slay, and so he wished them well and continued his journey.

The medicine man found the fourth Raven Mocker by sheer luck more than a week after he left his home. She was cunningly hidden in a cave near the outskirts of a small village way down in the valley. The villagers knew nothing of her presence, but people in the vicinity reported that the number of sudden or surprising deaths had significantly increased over the past two years. The elders had suspected the presence of a Raven Mocker but had been unable to locate it. The medicine man himself would have missed her, for she was a clever shape-shifter, but he had seen his arrow mark pulsing in her neck when she passed him, disguised as a local tribeswoman. There were too many people about for him to kill her at the time. Instead, he went to the village elders and told them what he had seen. Then he tracked the Raven Mocker back to her lair with two of the best hunters in the village.

One look into their eyes was enough to tell the withered old Raven Mocker that she was discovered. Before any of the men could react, the witch fell on her own knife rather than die at their hands.

"Bury her deep," the medicine man instructed the elders before departing again on his search.

He was gone more than a month from his home, but he did not find the two remaining Raven Mockers living in the region.

Admitting defeat at last, he returned home to his welcoming wife and reluctantly told the council of elders how he had fared.

"Four fewer witches to worry us?" they said to him. "You consider this defeat? Well done!"

They told him that the bodies of the male and female Raven Mockers he found the first day had been washed up in the stream in his absence. They were buried deep under a stone in a field outside the village.

The medicine man was uneasy and restless after returning to his home. He went about his daily tasks in an abstracted manner. The task still felt undone. But the remaining Raven Mockers were warned now of his sworn vengeance, and they did not appear in the village, even when two children came down with a high fever. Not a whoosh of wind or a raven scream did he hear, though he watched beside their beds for a day and a night.

He was preparing to leave the children's house on the morning of the third day, assuring their mother that they were both out of danger and would be fine with a few days' rest, when their young father returned home from his weeklong hunting trip. He was wild-eyed and panting as he burst into the room. "Raven Mockers," he gasped to the medicine man. "Two of them."

The medicine man's eyes widened in triumph. "Where? Tell me!"

Dropping into a crouch to ease the ache in his side, the hunter related his story. Dusk had overtaken him one night far from any village, but he had remembered seeing a house not far from the trail where an old man and his wife lived. No one was home when he arrived, so he had curled up in a corner and gone to sleep. He was awakened late at night by the cry of a raven,

Raven Mockers

and a moment later the old man came in and built a fire. The young hunter found something menacing in the scene and had remained still and silent as the old man took something out of a bundle and began roasting it over the coals. It looked like a man's heart.

Shortly thereafter, there came another sharp raven cry from outside, and then an old woman came in, frowning fiercely. "Did you have any luck?" her husband asked genially.

"None at all. There were too many holy men about," the woman grumbled.

"You never have any luck. Here, finish roasting this, and we will eat."

The woman bent over the fire for a time and then raised her head sharply. "Who is over in that corner?" she asked her husband.

"No one was there when I entered," he replied.

"And how would you know in the dark?" she asked. Rapidly they built up the fire. Alarmed, the young hunter feigned deep sleep, not responding to the loud noise they made at the fire, and only opening his eyes when the old man shook him. He rubbed his face and head and pretended great weariness as he spoke to his host.

Ignoring him, the wife hurried outside into the gray of predawn, and the young hunter heard her crying. He knew she was frightened because he might have overheard their conversation and identified them as Raven Mockers. If he had, their evil magic would turn against them, and they would perish. The young man hurried through the breakfast the old woman had prepared and exited the house as hastily as he could. The old man, hoping to bribe the hunter to forget anything he might have overheard, gave him a fancy piece of beadwork and a trumped-up explanation for his quarrel with the wife. At the next stream the hunter had thrown the beadwork away and had raced for home as fast as his legs would carry him.

He had traveled three and a half days since leaving that house, running as fast as he could, to summon the medicine men and the other tribal warriors. And they traveled three and a half days back to the place where the two remaining Raven Mockers lived.

It was exactly seven nights after the young hunter had overheard the Raven Mockers roasting a man's heart when the execution party reached their door. And true to their nature, the old man and woman lay dead on the floor of their house, killed by the evil spells that had once ruled them.

The medicine man ordered them burned with the entirety of their house and belongings. Then the hunters returned home, rejoicing that all the Raven Mockers in the range of their settlement had been destroyed.

Word of the medicine man who killed Raven Mockers spread throughout the Cherokee Nation. And Gunskali 'ski, the man who saw the invisible, was often called upon to sit with the sick and the dying and to hunt Raven Mockers from that day forward.

29

The Cat

EDENTON

I knew she was a witch the moment I laid eyes on her. At the time, I sat on the earthen dam beside my papa's mill with a fishing rod in my hand, and my mind on a tricky math problem I was trying to solve for school the next day. Then my eyes caught movement on the far side of the lake, and I saw the witch floating across the large millpond in a boat with no oars. There was no wind or stream to propel the boat forward, yet forward it came through the spring dusk that had fallen beneath the cyprus trees that surrounded our mill. The far side of the pond was a tangled forest dense with trees and underbrush. It was a darkly mysterious place, and no one ventured there because of the rumors that evil forces roamed the woods at night. Yet it was from this spot that the woman came to us in her magic boat.

Papa stood a few yards down from me, trying to catch us a catfish for dinner. He was watching the boat float toward us, but he didn't seem to notice that it had no oars or other means of propulsion. I thought his calm attitude strange at the time, not realizing he was already under the witch's spell.

In those days I was a precocious eleven-year-old tomboy with brains too big for my head, as Papa was fond of saying. I was in the advanced class at school, and my teacher told Papa I had a better vocabulary than a politician and ought to go to high school as soon as I reached a suitable age. In spite of my academic achievements, I spent all my free time running about in britches and ragtag flannel shirts with the sleeves rolled up, my brown hair hanging in two long braids over each shoulder. It was not uncommon for us to go fishing together, and sometimes Papa took me hunting too. Perhaps these were not womanly pursuits, but I had never cared about that—until the moment when the witch drew near the shore, and I saw her beautiful face under a stylish poke bonnet and beheld the wonderful dress she wore. I was filled instantly with jealousy. We could never afford such fancy clothing, even when the mill was working to capacity. My only dress was a worn gingham that was two sizes too small. I glared unhappily down at my britches and patched shirt, comparing them unfavorably with the witch's garb.

Then I forgot all about my clothes. Papa had stepped forward to help the woman ashore, and he looked like a stricken spaniel, all wide pleading eyes. He stammered when he spoke to her, and his face by turns went white and then flushed a bright red.

The witch spoke in a low, musical voice, explaining that she had journeyed a long way and lost her husband on the trip. She asked if we knew of a place she could spend the night. Judging from the look in Papa's eyes, I knew what his answer would be even before he spoke. He quickly offered up our cottage as a resting place, and she delicately accepted. Then, as an afterthought, he introduced me. We stared at each other for a moment, the witch and I. From the disdainful curl of her upper lip, I judged that she disapproved of my clothes. But she said all the right things, and Papa glared at me until I gave her a polite—if sullen—greeting.

The witch—who said her name was Faye—insisted on cooking dinner for us in exchange for our hospitality. Papa followed her every move with his stricken-spaniel look, taking in her glossy black hair, her red lips, her amber-colored eyes, and her hourglass figure. She smiled beguilingly at him as she served up his stew, and she laughed at his remarks even when he was not funny at all. It was a sickening display, but Papa lapped it up. When Faye came to put stew in my bowl, I flinched away. I couldn't help it. I already hated her for the spell she seemed to have over Papa. She glared at me, yellow sparks glowing in her amber eyes. But her red mouth kept smiling. Our eyes met for a moment, and in them I could see the future plainly. She was going to be my new mama, and God help me if I tried to interfere. She had years of experience and black magic on her side, and I was just a simple miller's daughter.

As Papa and Faye conversed that first evening, I wondered why she was bothering with him. He was a simple man, rough of speech and manner. His interests mainly lay in fishing and milling, and he did not get out much or care for the world outside our small town. Faye was well-spoken, well-read, and well-bred. They truly had nothing in common. But Faye wanted him, and that was that.

One night's stay turned into two, then three. A week passed. Then a month. And when the itinerant preacher made his stop in our town, Papa and Faye were married.

Things weren't too bad at first. Faye was polite to me when Papa was around, and when he worked in the mill, she ignored me. I was not important in her grand scheme of things, whatever that was. Of course, many of my daylight hours were spent in the local school, wearing my hated gingham dress and learning all the things Papa could not teach me—for his knowledge of academics was limited to the basic accounting and writing needed for his job at the mill. So I had no idea what Faye did during the hours I was away. But at nighttime she was coldly polite to me and cuddled in a sickeningly sweet manner with Papa.

I found it rather annoying to be considered so unimportant. Faye didn't even try to hide her magic from me when I returned each day from school. I'd swing through the cottage door with my heavy load of schoolbooks and find the broom sweeping itself across the floor or the laundry flying in through the window to fold itself neatly away in the dresser drawers. Faye would be preening herself in the small mirror she'd placed over our fireplace mantel the day she and Papa were married. She could not get enough of her own reflection and was as vain of her appearance as a pussycat. I would sit down at the kitchen table and do my homework while she languidly started dinner. The fire would burst into flame without her lifting a finger, and food would fly this way and that, chopping itself, setting itself into a pot or frying pan. But the magic always stopped abruptly a minute or two before Papa came home, and Faye would be bustling around the stove each night when the front door opened to admit her infatuated husband. Secretly, I rather admired the beautiful witch. I'd like to be able to command inanimate objects to perform for me. But having a good Christian upbringing, I knew that some evil price had to be paid for her to have gained such power. And I wasn't sure I wanted to pay such a price just to avoid housework.

I'm not sure when the change began. One morning, Faye had a hard time getting out of bed, and I was forced to fix breakfast for Papa and myself before leaving for school. Papa fretted that Faye was sickening for something, but to my jaundiced eye it looked as if Faye had gone out late at night and not returned until dawn. In that moment I got an inkling of why Faye had married my father. His mill was ideally situated at the edge of the great woods where the evil witches and other dark creatures were said to conduct their grim deeds. She could easily participate in nightly revels and have a warm, comfortable, safe place to lodge during the day.

I said nothing to Papa of my speculations. I'd tried to tell Papa that he had married a witch, but he had scolded me soundly and had threatened to thrash me if I spoke such things in the town. So I kept my mouth shut. He was too far gone under Faye's spell to believe a word I said.

Around midsummer Papa went away on a hunting trip and insisted that Faye and I stay at the neighbors' farm until he returned. This was not a good idea. Within a day or two of our arrival, I overheard the neighbor's wife telling her husband that Faye's bed had only a small, cat-size hollow in the mattress when she went to make it each morning after breakfast, rather than the large hollow typically made by a full-grown human. The husband and wife exchanged significant looks when she said this, but they spoke no more of the matter at the time, for Faye chose that moment to trip happily into the room with a huge bouquet of flowers in her arms, freshly picked from the fields outside the farm.

Several times during that visit, I heard Faye creeping out of the farmhouse at night. She never returned before dawn. The farmer's wife heard her too, and she nodded significantly to her husband when Faye missed breakfast two days in a row and spent most of the afternoon napping. They looked pityingly at me, and the farmer—a round, jolly old man with a shock of white hair, a broad red face, and peppermints in his pockets—told me that I was welcome to stay at their house anytime, should the need arise. That was as far as they would go in expressing their opinion of my father's wife. At least to me. In town they were far more candid. By the time Papa arrived home from his trip, everyone in Edenton was convinced that he had married a witch.

Papa was furious when the rumors reached his ears. He would not believe me when I told him that I had nothing to do with the "vicious talk," and he thrashed me soundly with a willow switch until I could not sit down at supper. He wouldn't speak to me that night, or for much of the following week, as business at the mill slacked off because of the rumors. In the house Faye spent much of the day sleeping, becoming her vivacious self only after the evening meal. And she neglected the chores—not even bothering to clean with her magic. I found myself cooking and cleaning and doing any number of housewifely tasks just to keep our little home running.

Meanwhile, things at the mill were going wrong for Papa. The grinding wheels that mashed the grain to powder started sparking and jerking strangely, and he had to stop his work to fix them. The next day, he found nails in the grain hopper.

And the day after that, he found many sacks of corn slashed open and grain spilled everywhere. Papa scolded me furiously that evening, sure that my "nasty talk" had encouraged the neighbors to play tricks on him. I cowered away from him, afraid of my own father for the first time in my life. His rough face was dark red and contorted with anger. Surprisingly, it was Faye herself who intervened, saying languidly, "What does it matter, my dear? We are above such childish tricks. Who cares if the peasants talk?"

Her words mollified my father, at least long enough for me to escape outdoors. My shaking legs took me down the lane to the farmer's house without my mind engaging in a conscious choice. The farmer's wife saw me coming and flung the door wide so that she could embrace me, murmuring soothing words until my sobs had ceased. Her husband hovered protectively around us, and he pressed several peppermints into my hands and called me his good girl as I poured out my woeful tale. I told them everything—from Faye's arrival in the magic boat to my beating and the terrible things happening at Papa's mill. If I was going to be blamed for all the witch talk in town, then I may as well talk!

The farmer's wife urged her husband to speak to Papa on my behalf, and he agreed to do so the very next day. Reassured by their calm manner, I wiped my eyes, ate some peppermints, and went home. It was dark when I arrived home, and the house was empty. Papa's absence was easily explained. He always went to the country store to play checkers with the other men on Wednesday evenings. But Faye was usually home.

I went over to the fire and added a few logs and then lit the lantern. Outside, the wind had sprung up, and I heard the growl of thunder. A storm was coming. I listened uneasily as the thunder grew nearer and the wind grew louder. I went to fetch the sweater I was knitting for Papa and tried to concentrate on it, but I kept dropping stitches. I kept wondering if the dam gate was open. A sudden storm such as this one might cause flooding, and that could easily wash out the mill. With Papa away at the country store and Faye gone to whatever witches' Sabbath she attended at night, it was up to me to protect the mill.

A sudden downpour thundered against the roof of the cottage. I shuddered with dread at the sound. If this kept up, the mill *would* be in danger. I shrugged into my coat and hurried outside with my lantern. I was instantly drenched, and the wind howled so fiercely around me that I staggered, the light of the lantern bobbing wildly in my hand. And that's when I saw the black cats swarming around the door of the mill. There were more than a dozen of them, and they were huge cats—almost the size of cougars—with blazing eyes and bristling tails. They batted at the mill door with giant paws until it fell open. I gaped at them. They must be witches' familiars, I decided. But why were they interested in our mill? I could see through the open doorway and realized that they were circling around something in the mill. What mischief were the creatures planning?

I crept cautiously to the closest window, rose on tiptoe, and looked inside. To my horror, I saw my father standing in the center of a rapidly tightening circle of giant black cats. He hadn't gone to the country store at all. He had been lying in wait for the vandals who were sabotaging the mill. And he had found more than he had bargained for.

The huge cats swiped at him with their long claws. I saw bloody tears in his shirt, and one leg of his pants was hanging down in back, nearly ripped off by a black cat with blazing amber eyes. As I watched, Papa swung at it desperately with his axe.

There was no way he could hold them all off on his own, I realized, glancing around for a weapon I could use to help defend my father. Seeing a long stick on the nearby woodpile, I grabbed it and charged toward the door of the mill.

At that moment, there came a tremendous caterwauling from inside. I was knocked sprawling by a dozen wailing cats that came bursting through the mill door. They were followed a moment later by my father, who dropped his axe into the mud as he clutched the doorpost for balance. He was dazed and injured. I rolled upright, intent on reaching him and helping him to safety. But he revived suddenly and staggered down the path toward the cottage. I shouted to him, but my call was drowned out by the thunderous rain. So I raced after him, fighting the rain and the heavy wind. Please God, let him be all right!

As I slammed open the front door, I heard Papa shout with horror from his bedroom. I gasped and ran toward the bedroom door. Then I froze in shock. Papa was staring disbelievingly at Faye, who lay bleeding on the bed. One of her arms had been severed at the wrist. "You!" he cried in a voice of such anguish that it wrung my heart. "You were the cat with the amber eyes that injured me? You, who I took into my heart and into my home?"

"Yes, me, you silly fool. Me! Why else would I stay with such a common fellow as you, except to be near my brethren?" Faye screamed. And she transformed suddenly into a huge black cat with blazing amber eyes and leapt at him, sharp claws extending from her three remaining paws. Papa dodged out of the way,

211

and I ducked as the witch cat leapt right over me and raced out the front door.

Papa turned to stare at me, his eyes huge with horror. "Oh, little girl! Oh, my baby. I'm so sorry," he gasped. "I beat you, and all the time you were telling me the truth."

Tears sprang to my eyes. Papa already looked different, as if the witch's spell had been broken at last. I reached out to him, and he swept me into his arms, apologizing over and over for bringing Faye into our house.

It was at this moment that we both heard a sudden watery roar from the stream that fed the millpond. We'd heard that terrible sound once before, and it had nearly destroyed our mill. It was a flash flood!

My eyes widened. "Papa! I didn't have time to open the dam gate. I was distracted by the black cats!"

"Stay here," Papa said quickly. "I'll go."

"But you're injured," I shouted after him. He was already gone through the open door into the pounding rain. I raced after him, ignoring his injunction. His legs were much longer than mine, and he quickly outdistanced me. I saw him run out along the dam; saw the huge wave of water hit it; saw the dam shudder with the impact and dissolve into nothingness, throwing my father into the swirling nightmare of the flash flood.

I screamed. I ran along the bank of the pond, searching desperately for a glimpse of my father. I saw nothing but swirling, muddy water and the debris from the dam. Finally, I ran down the lane, bursting in on the sleeping farmer and his wife, shouting desperately for assistance. The farmer came at once, while his wife roused the other neighbors.

THE CAT

Everyone searched along the shore of the large pond in the pouring rain, the bravest venturing on the side closest to the witch woods. The pond had overflowed its banks in the flash flood, making the search difficult. But we kept trying to find my father, hoping he'd been washed ashore somewhere. I wanted to haul out the rowboat and search on the water, but no one would let me. The millpond churned wickedly under the storm surge. No boat would survive the maelstrom at its center. No boat and no person, I realized, my tears mixing with the rain soaking my cheeks.

The farmer's wife took me home and tucked me into bed, giving me hot tea to drink and whispering soothingly to me until I fell asleep. My dreams were full of black cats, severed arms, and Faye's dancing broom, punctuated by my father's final scream as the dam broke underneath him.

It took them two days to find my father's drowned body at the far end of the pond, near the witch woods from which Faye had emerged in her magic boat. Tangled up in his clothes, they found the severed paw of a black cat.

There isn't much else to tell. The farmer and his wife took me in and raised me as their own. I went on to high school and eventually married my sweetheart and settled down in Edenton. I never went back to the mill, though, close as it was to my new home. The memories there were too painful, even now.

But I still sometimes wonder what happened to Faye.

30

The Cursed Quilt

Bertha was not my favorite relative. She was bold as brass, with a sharp tongue and a bullying manner that did not endear her to me. Worse, she turned coy and sweet around boys and adults, hiding her true colors behind a false front. So when she moved in with my family after her folks passed, I was not pleased. Bertha was older than the rest of us, and she bossed us around something cruel. Mama saw through her conniving, but Papa was completely taken in.

All us girls shared a room, and Bertha and I had to sleep in the same bed. I ended up with twelve inches of space and Bertha took the rest. Anytime I tried to claim more territory, she'd kick me until I moved, pretending all the while that she was fast asleep.

As soon as I was old enough, I got work in the local mercantile. The owners offered to provide room and board as well as my wage, so I stayed in town during the week and went home for Sunday dinner. It was a relief to get away from Bertha, but I couldn't figure out why she didn't take the job herself. It was a fine opportunity for a girl from a poor family, but Bertha let the position go to me. I figured she preferred bossing the young 'uns over doing an honest day's work. But it turned out she had something else in mind.

Folks shopping at the mercantile started gossiping about Bertha and the preacher's boy. He'd been going with a girl named Bess for nearly a year, but dropped her as soon as Bertha looked his way. Lord almighty, I was furious. Bess was a nice girl and didn't deserve to be thrown over for someone like Bertha.

I heard that Bess was heartbroken and had pleaded with Bertha to let the preacher's son go. Bertha, of course, had refused. There was some speculation that Bess might be in the family way, so devastated was she by the whole situation.

Before a month had passed, Bertha and the preacher's boy were engaged to wed. Her future papa-in-law looked embarrassed when he made the announcement on Sunday. Bess started crying softly into her handkerchief and her Mama took her away. Her Granny, who was the town herbalist and healer, sat stiff and disapproving in the pew, glaring at the preacher and his son. But she turned all soft and sweet when she met Bertha in the churchyard after the sermon.

"Congratulations to ye," she said, taking Bertha's hand into her gnarled grip. "I'm making ye a quilt for yer new household."

Bertha smirked and tossed her blond curls. "That is right kind of you, Granny," she said and winked at me over the old lady's shoulder.

Two weeks later, Granny brought a pink and green quilt to church with her and presented it to Bertha. "The pattern's called Catch My Breath," Granny told Bertha. "It's a wedding quilt, so you must sleep under it every night to dream of your true love. And it will add spice to the marriage bed, if'n you know what I mean."

Bertha cooed over the quilt and showed it to everyone, including Bess. When we got home after church, she went right to our room and tucked it carefully on her side of the bed.

It was a lovely quilt, all soft blues and pinks. I'd never seen the pattern before. It was full of circles and oblongs made out of many small triangles. If you looked at it just right, it looked like a menacing face with an open mouth full of sharp teeth. There was a faint smell of herbs coming from the quilt. I smelled tansy, rue, mugwort, and pennyroyal. Those were strange herbs to give to a bride. I shivered suddenly.

"I've never heard of a Catch My Breath quilt," I said. "I still don't understand why Bess's grandmother would give you a wedding quilt."

"She probably invented the pattern just for me," Bertha said smugly, tossing her curls. "And she gave me the quilt so everyone would know I am a much better match for the preacher's son than silly old Bess."

She walked away with her nose in the air. I sighed and went down to help Mama with the Sunday dinner.

I was shocked when I saw Bertha at church the next week. She was pale and there were dark rings under her eyes. Her perky blonde curls were drooping and there were lines around her lips.

"What's wrong with Bertha?" I whispered to Mama during the first hymn.

"She ain't sleeping too good," Mama told me. "Hush now. We'll talk after dinner."

Bertha was her usual bossy self in the churchyard, but I couldn't help noticing that she walked kind of stiff on the way back to the cove.

"She's been having nightmares," Mama told me after dinner as we washed up the dishes. "Says a black cat comes and lays on her chest each night. She wakes up screaming and gasping for breath."

"You don't reckon . . . " I paused, wondering how much to say. Mama raised an eyebrow at me. "You don't reckon it's that Catch My Breath quilt Granny gave her, bringing on the dreams?"

"Pshaw, it ain't nothing of the sort. It's bridal nerves, I expect," Mama said. "The wedding's only a few weeks away and there's so much to do to get ready to set up housekeeping. I don't know how we are going to be ready in time."

Mama was right about all the work. Every minute I wasn't at the mercantile, I was sewing napkins for Bertha's hope chest or making lace or running errands. It was a real whirlwind of activity. Bertha didn't seem to be doing much of the work herself, except standing for fittings for her fancy wedding dress. She seemed paler each time I saw her. The lines on her face grew more pronounced and she held herself at a funny angle as if her back hurt her. Mama said she still had nightmares about a black cat that sat on her chest and pressed the air out of her. A couple of times, Mama found Bertha with her head all wrapped up in the quilt. "It's no wonder she feels like she can't breathe," Mama scolded. "I keep telling her to tuck it in before she goes to sleep at night. But half the time she doesn't remember."

"I think you should take that quilt away from her, Mama," I said. "I think it's cursed."

But Mama didn't believe in curses. And Bertha was so proud of that quilt that she wouldn't listen to me when I told her that I thought the quilt was causing the dreams. "You're just jealous.

The Cursed Quilt

And you're right to be. I'm getting married and you'll be an old maid," she jeered.

The wedding day arrived and we helped Bertha do her hair up nice. The fancy dress looked real fine, but Bertha wasn't at her best. She was too thin, there was no color in her face, and her curls had lost their bounce. But she was as coy and bossy as ever, and the look of dawning terror on the preacher boy's face when she marched down the aisle and took his arm told me he'd finally realized what he was getting into.

During the wedding supper, I sought out Granny. "Where is Bess?" I asked her. "I haven't seen her in town."

"Bess is staying with her cousin," Granny said. "There's a nice farmer in that village who would make a good husband." And father. Neither of us said it, but we both understood.

I reached into my pocket and pulled out a lace-edged handkerchief that I'd made while I was doing all the extra sewing for Bertha's wedding.

"It's a gift for Bess. I hope everything comes right for her," I said, handing it to Granny.

"I'll be sure she gets it," Granny said. "Thank ye."

We gave Bertha and her new husband a rousing send-off. They were staying in a remote hunting cabin for their honeymoon, before returning to set up housekeeping in a small cabin behind the preacher's house. Bertha took the new quilt with her, since Granny had hinted it would make the marriage bed even sweeter.

No one heard anything from the happy couple for several days. We figured they'd decided to extend their honeymoon, so no one was worried, though more than one ribald remark was made. After a week, the preacher and Papa decided enough

219

The Cursed Quilt

was enough. The couple must be getting low on food and you couldn't live on nothing but love and air. They went to the hunting cabin to visit the newlyweds and ask them to come home. When they stepped inside, they found Bertha and the preacher's boy dead on the bed, the wedding quilt wrapped tightly around their throats.

31

The Man in Gold

HIGH POINT

There was once a very proud girl who lived in a huge mansion in Guilford County. Her father doted upon his daughter and indulged her whenever he could. When she stated that she was not going to marry any man unless he came to her dressed all in gold, her father made no objection. The girl's little brother, who was very wise, told her that she would live to regret her rash words. But the daughter just laughed at him.

One evening, the father and mother gave a fancy ball for their daughter. Everyone who was anyone attended.

The daughter danced and laughed and flirted with all the young men. But none of them caught her fancy.

Her little brother, bored with the party, went down to the gate to talk with the coachmen. While he was there, a fancy carriage, driven by a hooded, featureless man and pulled by four fine black horses, stopped at the gate. A handsome man, dressed all in gold, stepped out of the carriage.

"I am here to see the man of the house on business," the elegant man said to the gatekeeper. The little brother watched the man from behind the gate. There was something not quite right about the man in gold, but he could not put his finger on what was wrong. The gatekeeper, awed by the fancy carriage, the fine black horses, and the gold clothing, let the man in at once.

As the man entered the courtyard, the little brother bowed to him and said, "I will take you to my father."

The father was pleased to meet the elegant man dressed in gold.

"It seems I have interrupted a ball," the man in gold said after they had been introduced. "I could come back at another time."

"Oh no, sir. Please join us. My daughter would like to meet you," said the father.

Indeed, the daughter was thrilled to meet the handsome man dressed in gold. She abandoned all the other young men and would dance with no one else the rest of the evening. The little brother stayed in the ballroom, studying the elegant man partnering his sister. Something was not quite right about the man. Then the little brother noticed that the elegant man's boots were too small for his size, as if his legs ended in something other than feet. Yet he danced with grace and skill.

Between dance sets, the little brother said to his sister, "Sister, did you notice the man's feet?"

"What about his feet?" asked the daughter lazily, waving her fan and watching the man in gold pouring her a drink of lemonade.

"His boots are too small and yet he dances as if his feet were normal. You should ask him about it."

"Ask him yourself," said the daughter as her escort came back with her drink.

"What is it you wish to ask me?" inquired the man in gold.

"What is wrong with your feet?" asked the little brother.

The elegant man raised an eyebrow, then frowned as if he thought the boy's question impertinent. But he answered it. "When I was a child, I fell into the fire and my feet were partially burned off. Fortunately, I overcame my handicap."

The man in gold bowed to the daughter and swept her onto the dance floor. The little brother frowned. It seemed to him that there was still something wrong. He studied the man in gold intently. The man's hands looked rather strange. They were gnarled and red, with very long nails that looked like claws. When the man and the sister returned to their chairs for a short rest, the brother said to the man, "Did you burn your hands too?"

"Really, brother!" His sister was annoyed. "That is rude. Apologize immediately."

The little brother apologized, and the man in gold graciously accepted his apology. But the man's eyes were cold, and the little brother felt it was prudent to leave the couple alone.

By the end of the ball, the man in gold and the daughter of the house were betrothed. The man, impatient to claim his bride, told the parents that he would take her to his home where they would be married. The parents were dazzled by the man's obvious wealth and agreed to let their daughter go away with him. The daughter, though completely infatuated by the man in gold, was a bit nervous about marrying in such haste.

"I will go with you gladly, sir," she said. "But I am going to a strange place and wish to have someone from my family accompany me. Little brother, will you come?"

The little brother agreed at once. He did not like the man in gold and did not want his sister to marry the man. The man had his carriage brought around, and he settled his bride-to-be and her brother inside. The little brother looked out the window and saw the man in gold toss an egg into the air. It transformed into a large bird.

"Hop and skip, Betty. Go along and prepare the road for us," the man said.

The large bird flew away. The man stepped into the carriage, and the featureless coachman drove them out the gate and down the road in the direction the large bird had flown. The man in gold was silent, gazing out at the dark night. The daughter took her little brother's hand. Her fingers were shaking. The little brother squeezed his sister's hand and looked carefully around the carriage, seeking something to aid them should they need it. He saw a grubby sack underneath the seat across from them, where the man in gold sat. Otherwise, the carriage was empty.

Ahead of the carriage, a glow appeared on the horizon. It grew brighter and brighter as the carriage drove toward it. Smoke filled the air and blew into the carriage. The daughter and her brother started coughing.

"Sir, we cannot go that way. There is a fire," said the daughter.

"That is just my men burning off new ground for my crops," the man in gold said impatiently.

"Please sir, we cannot breathe through this smoke. We must turn aside," said the daughter. She was very nervous now. The man in gold was looking less and less like a handsome man the closer they got to the fire.

"I will check to see if there is a clear passage," the man in gold said. He asked the coachman to stop, swept up the grubby sack, and stepped out of the carriage.

The little brother saw him take an egg out of the sack and throw it up in the air. It transformed into a large bird.

"Hop and skip, Betty," the man said. "Clear the smoke for our passage home."

He stood watching as the large bird flew toward the fire.

"Brother, I am scared," said the daughter as they watched the man out the window.

"Sister, you should be scared. That is no man. That is the devil."

The little brother reached under the opposite seat, searching for something he could use against the man in gold. He found an egg that had rolled out of the grubby sack.

"Come sister," said the little brother. He pulled his sister out the door on the far side of the carriage. Then the little brother threw the egg into the air. The egg transformed into a large bird.

"Hop and skip, Betty," said the little brother. "Carry us home."

At once the huge bird picked them up in its claws and flew the brother and sister back to their parents' home.

The daughter was very glad to be back home. She wept and told her parents the whole story. They were grateful that their children had escaped. But the little brother was not so sure they had escaped. While the parents led their daughter to her bed to rest, her brother slipped down to the village to talk to May Brown, the local wisewoman.

After May Brown heard the little brother's tale, she nodded her head. "That bird will fly right back to the devil, and the devil will know your sister has returned to her home. The devil will come for her, since she is promised to him in marriage."

"What should we do then?" asked the little brother.

"I will engage the devil in a riddle contest," said the wisewoman. "If I win, then the devil will leave your sister alone. If I lose, then she will have to marry him and go to live with him in General Cling Town."

"What's General Cling Town?" asked the little brother.

"General Cling Town is what we wisewomen call hell," said May Brown soberly, "because the devil 'clings' to people, tempting them to do wrong, and is generally hard to remove."

Just then, they heard a thunderous cry of rage that echoed through the whole sky. There was the sound of hooves racing toward the mansion.

"The devil is coming," said the wisewoman. She took the little brother by the hand. They hurried up to the mansion, meeting the devil in his black chariot as he came driving away from the house, the daughter cowering beside him. He looked nothing like a man now. He was glowing red with wicked black eyes, horns on his head, and cloven feet.

The devil pulled the horses to a stop when he saw them. His eyes met those of the local wisewoman. The little brother could tell at once that they knew each other. When she saw them, the daughter begged them to save her.

"Is anyone here? Anyone here?" the devil said softly, his eyes glittering. "Name of May Brown from General Cling Town."

"I am here," said the wisewoman. "My name is May Brown, but I am not from General Cling Town."

"What is whiter than any sheep's down in General Cling Town?" asked the devil.

"Snow," said the wise woman. "Snow is whiter than any sheep's down in General Cling Town."

The devil glared at her.

The Man in Gold

"What is greener than any wheat grown in General Cling Town?" he asked.

"Grass," said the wisewoman. "Grass is greener than any wheat grown in General Cling Town."

"What is bluer than anything down in General Cling Town?"

"The sky is bluer than anything down in General Cling Town," said the wisewoman.

The devil was furious. He was only allowed four riddles, and May Brown had answered the first three correctly.

"What is louder than any horns down in General Cling Town?" asked the Devil.

"Thunder is louder than any horns down in General Cling Town," said the wisewoman. The little brother knew the wisewoman had answered correctly, and so did the devil. He hopped up and down in his chariot, beside himself with rage. The devil had lost his bride.

"I will have your soul for this, May Brown," shouted the devil.

May Brown removed her shoe, tore off the sole, and threw it to the devil.

The devil caught the sole in his hands. He gripped it so hard it started to burn. The devil stared at it in disbelief. The devil thought he could claim May Brown's soul, but she had tricked him by giving him the sole of her shoe!

The devil howled, a chilling sound that haunted the little brother's dreams for the rest of his life. Then the devil threw the daughter out of his carriage. She landed at her brother's feet. The devil tossed an egg into the air. It transformed into a large bird.

"Hop and skip, Betty. Take me home," said the devil.

And with that, the devil disappeared.

32

The Ghost Club

ASHEVILLE

It all started with the newspaper article. Nathaniel was reading in his usual spot on the steps of the schoolhouse while the rest of us threw a ball around the yard after lunch. Nathaniel's Pa was a big man in the railroad business. He traveled a lot and brought home newspapers from everywhere he went for his intellectual son. Nathaniel faithfully read them during the lunch hour while the rest of us were relaxing.

The girls were gathered in their usual group, talking and laughing. Mary kept catching my eye, and whenever she did, I dropped the ball and the other fellows jeered at me. I flushed and vowed to keep my eye on the ball, but then Mary looked at me again and I never even noticed it flying over my head.

Before I could retrieve the ball, a bellow interrupted our sport.

"Fellows!" Nathaniel shouted. He was waving his father's old newspaper over his head like a wild man as he ran toward us. "Fellows! Look at this article about Crawfordsville, Indiana."

"Why should we care about Crawfordsville Indiana?" one fellow asked.

"Because they have a Ghost Club," Nathaniel said excitedly.

That got our attention. Everyone, even the girls, hurried over to see his newspaper. It was a long article, so Nathaniel summed it up for us. Apparently, a group in Crawfordsville had formed a club whose membership had one single requirement: The members must have personally seen a ghost at least once in their lives. The club was formed on October 31—All Hallows Eve—and each year they indoctrinated new members. They met regularly to tell true ghost stories in a building that itself had several hauntings. Several of their ghostly tales were related in the article, but before we could read any of them, Nathaniel folded the paper under his arms and said, "I think we should do it!"

"Do what?" asked a girl suspiciously.

"I think we should form our own Society for Advancement of Belief in Ghosts," Nathaniel said patiently.

"How can we? We've never seen a ghost," a boy pointed out skeptically.

"I have," said Nathaniel promptly. "My granny is Scottish, and I was born with her sixth sense."

"I have too," I said at once. Well, it was probably a sheet flapping on a windy night, but since I never went to check before running for the house, I figure it could have been a ghost.

"I live in a haunted house," Mary volunteered. "My father's sister fell down the staircase the night before her wedding and broke her neck. Her ghost is said to haunt the staircase and the front parlor."

The schoolyard was suddenly filled with young scholars vying to tell their personal ghost stories. Alas, the bell rang at that moment, and we were called back to class. But not before a bunch of us agreed to meet after school to discuss the Ghost

Club. The upshot of that meeting was the inauguration of the Asheville Ghost Club on All Hallows Eve, which was a week away.

Mary's parents were spiritualists and were happy to host our first club meeting in their haunted home. The whole family pitched in to turn their front parlor into a spooky masterpiece that rivaled the description in Nathaniel's newspaper. On All Hallows Eve, every member of our class showed up on Mary's doorstep at the appointed hour; even Gregory who claimed he'd spent a night in a haunted graveyard in order to qualify for the club. His tale of a misty figure rising from a grave was probably as real as my haunted sheet, but there was no way either of us were missing out on this club.

Mary looked pretty as a picture standing in the doorway greeting all her classmates. She blushed when I complimented her dress and fluttered her eyelashes when she told me she'd saved me a seat. She ushered us into the parlor, which was deliciously creepy. White cheesecloth hung from the ceiling and draped the walls. The posh furnishings had been replaced with rows of chairs covered in black cloth that faced a massive table in front of the fireplace. On the table lay a bell, a prayer book, and a candle to lay any ghosts that were raised that night, in accordance with the tenets of ghost lore. There were skeletons in each corner with red lanterns that lit up the mouth and eye sockets in a suitably gruesome manner.

The spooky atmosphere within the shadowy room gave me goosebumps. Or maybe it was the presence of Mary by my side. Her parents welcomed us to their home before retiring to the dining room to chaperone from a discreet distance.

Nathaniel took his place behind the table. We had already elected him club president, so he brought us to order and explained the rules drawn up for our club and the meeting schedule. He'd even written out a charter for us to sign.

After the formalities were concluded, we took a short break before regrouping for the main event. According to our new club rules, there would be two formal presentations per meeting. Each speaker would tell a true ghost story that they themselves had experienced. After the stories were concluded, they would answer questions and we would have a group discussion before closing with cake and refreshments. Nathaniel and Mary had volunteered to be the first two presenters.

Nathaniel resumed his place behind the table and began his ghost story. "When I was seven, my parents took me to a box supper at the church. It was a lovely evening, so we decided to walk since the sanctuary wasn't far from our house. The church was packed with families and there were lots of children my age running around having a great time."

Nathaniel paused for a sip of water, then continued. "At first, I didn't notice the barefoot little girl in the white dress. She was much younger than me—maybe four or five—and she wasn't from any of the families with which we were acquainted. She started following me as I went from table to table to talk with my friends. And she followed me outside when a bunch of us wanted to run races to get out the energy from all the pies and cakes we'd eaten. She watched so wistfully that I considered asking her to play with us. But my buddies thought girls were nuisances and wouldn't have been polite. So I ignored her, hoping she'd go back to her family or find some girls to play with."

Nathaniel tugged on his fingers as if he still felt guilty for ignoring the little girl. "It was getting dark, so my parents gathered our things and we said good night to our friends. By the time we left the church, I had forgotten all about the barefoot little girl in white. It was only when we turned onto the road that led to our home that I saw her shyly following us. I stopped and pointed sternly back to the church. 'Go back to your family, little girl. They will be missing you,' I said. My parents turned to look at me. 'Who are you talking to, Nathaniel?' asked my mother. I pointed toward the little girl, who was standing a couple feet away. She watched us with interest and gave no sign of wanting to leave. 'I'm talking to that little girl. She followed me around during the box supper and she won't go back to the church. Her parents will be worried.'"

Nathaniel took another swallow of water. His face was several shades paler than normal and the paper from which he was reading shook in his hands. "My father frowned and said: 'I do not see anyone standing there, Nathaniel.' And suddenly, neither did I."

Everyone in the room gasped.

"The barefoot little girl had vanished without a trace. I'd been followed all evening by a ghost," Nathaniel confirmed our suspicions. "I gasped and started shaking all over with fright. My parents, to their credit, believed my story at once. They took me home and put me to bed with a glass of warm milk. My father went back to the church to ask if anyone knew about the ghost of a little girl that haunted the place. The pastor told him that a little girl fitting his description had been killed in a carriage accident in front of the sanctuary. She was buried in the churchyard. Her parents moved away from Asheville, but her cousins still lived in town and claimed that they often saw the little girl in the churchyard, watching other children play."

We clapped vigorously at the conclusion of Nathaniel's tale, but our enthusiasm did little to dispel the gloomy menace that enveloped the room. The red light emanating from the skull's eye sockets flickered, making the shadows around us dance. The air felt so cold, I expected ice crystals to form in front of my nose each time I breathed out.

When the clapping ceased, a pale young woman stepped to the front of the room. She was wearing a long white gown that nearly blended with the cheesecloth hangings around the room. Her presence seemed to cast a spell over the room. She was unknown to us, but we did not question her appearance. Indeed, we were all mesmerized as she told her tale.

"It was an arranged marriage," the woman began. "Two prominent local families decided to unite their lineage. The son of a penniless nobleman was marrying the eldest daughter of a rich merchant. Thus, the middle-class family gained prestige and the nobleman's family procured a fortune."

The pale woman's voice was sibilant and strange. Icy chills were running up and down my spine. Mary's clasp on my hand grew so tight I lost the sensation in my fingers.

"The merchant's daughter loved the noble heir. He was darkly handsome with flashing eyes and a roguish grin. His courtship was dashing and outwardly sincere. He brought her flowers and expensive gifts. He wooed her with pretty words. Everything on the surface seemed perfect and a grand wedding was planned. But something was not right. The girl's brother was concerned. The heir had been seen several times around town, flirting with the daughter of a lawyer who had just moved to Asheville."

The pale woman paused. The room was so still you could hear the wind whistling outside the window. It was a lonely sound.

"The wedding invitations were sent, the wedding gown purchased, the paperwork uniting the family fortunes signed. There was no backing out of the marriage, no matter how many lawyers' daughters moved to town," the pale woman said. "In spite of her brother's concern, the merchant's daughter was hopeful. She was a beautiful girl herself and she was sure the noble heir loved her. To ease her brother's mind, she sent a note to the heir asking him to meet her at the house. It was the eve of her wedding and therefore unlucky for the groom to see his bride. Knowing the family would object to this lapse in tradition, she asked the heir to meet her upstairs in a private sitting room where they could talk without being disturbed. There, the merchant's daughter asked the heir about the other woman. The heir's eyes flashed with anger at her words, and the truth spilled out. He did not love her. He had never loved her. If it weren't for the money, he would never marry her."

An indignant rustle passed through the room. The pale woman waited until it subsided to continue.

"The heir stormed out of the room and the merchant's daughter followed, threatening to break their engagement and nullify the agreement between their families. The heir and the merchant's daughter stood face-to-face at the top of the staircase, glaring at each other. Then a cruel smile crossed the heir's face. 'You will never break our engagement,' he told the merchant's daughter and pushed her down the stairs. When she lay crumpled and broken at the bottom, the heir slipped away unnoticed. No one ever knew he had been in the house the night the merchant's daughter died."

Someone gasped and we all turned to see Mary's father standing in the doorway of the dining room. "Maud?" he whispered, staring in disbelief at the pale woman. "Maud, is that true? Did Henry kill you?"

My eyes widened as his words registered in my mind. I stared in shock as I realized that the pale woman standing beside the massive table was a ghost.

"Henry pushed me down the stairs on the eve of our wedding," Maud's spirit confirmed. "There was a clause in the marriage agreement that said the money would go to the heir if I died before the wedding, provided the engagement was not broken. When I threatened to end our betrothal, Henry knew the only way to keep the money was to kill me. So that is what he did."

"The scoundrel. The reprobate!" Mary's father was incoherent with rage.

"Tell our father the truth," Maud said. "That is all I ask." Her pale body grew translucent and then faded slowly away.

There was a moment of stunned silence. Then my classmates screamed, and a mass exodus ensued. Within moments, there was not a soul left in the room save Mary, her father, and me.

Mary's father sank into a black-draped chair. He was trembling from head to toe.

"What will you do, sir?" I asked, since Mary seemed incapable of speech.

"I will tell my father the truth," Mary's father said. "There's nothing we can do about the marriage agreement. Without proof of the murder, it is impossible to break. It is our word against Henry's.

"And it happened so many years ago that Henry and his family are long returned to England." He rubbed a trembling hand over his face, looking lost and sorrowful.

THE GHOST CLUB

"I think Aunt Maud just wanted us to know the truth," Mary said, hurrying over to hug her father.

I helped the family clean up the front parlor before taking my leave. Mary walked me to the front door.

"Well, no one will ever forget the first meeting of the Ghost Club," I said as stepped out into the chilly air of All Hallows Eve.

"Do you think there will be a second meeting?" she asked dryly.

"Heavens, I hope not," I said sincerely. "I don't need any more convincing. Aunt Maud's ghost was a real as they come."

The next day at school, Nathaniel tore up the charter and we unanimously agreed that the gathering on All Hallows Eve was the first and only meeting of the Asheville Ghost Club. Rest in peace, Aunt Maud.

33

A Tremendous Leap

FRANKLIN

It was a lackluster ghost story at best, I decided as I took another pull on my beer. Honestly, I had heard children's tales that sounded scarier! But the local men clustered around the bar told the tale as if it were gospel truth. I had trouble keeping a straight face.

According to the local dwellers, a giant had been inhabiting a local bald many years ago and the monster had caused great suffering among the villagers who lived at the foot of the mountain. There was much rejoicing when a rockslide felled the giant during a storm, but joy turned to fear when the apparition of the monster began haunting a winding narrow road near the village. Shortly thereafter, a troop of smaller spirits appeared in the same lane and accosted the giant in their midst. It was assumed by the village folk that these were victims of the late-giant, come to avenge themselves upon their murderer. The road being a major connector of two communities, these spirits made much trouble for locals traveling to and fro.

It was my good fortune (or not) that I was staying the week at the inn closest to this narrow road. For several evenings in a row, I'd heard retellings of the local ghost story. Sadly, if I were to summarize all the stories into a single sentence, it would be: "I saw the ghosts and they scared me, so I hurried away." Truly, not much of a tale.

Up until now, the stories had all been hearsay. Someone's cousin or nephew or son had encountered the ghost. But this evening, a tall, bearded man with solemn gray eyes spoke up. He was a farrier whose work took him all over the mountain, and he had seen these phantoms firsthand. I studied the man's face as he spoke of the spirits. One misty figure dominated the track until several smaller apparitions rose from the underbrush and overwhelmed him; the whole kit and caboodle at last vanished into the mountain. The farrier spoke so matter-of-factly that I almost believed his story, even though giants—to my mind— were not real.

As the talk in the bar turned to an intricate local romance, I remembered the giant tales I had learned as a child. Jack the Giant Killer was a story my granny often told at bedtime. As a boy, I had played the heroic Jack at a hospital fundraiser. At the climax of the story, I had faced down the giant ogre and executed a flying leap through a fake second story window to escape the monster's wrath. A small group of men holding a blanket caught me behind the scenes and restored me to my feet unharmed. No one in the audience knew of this fail-safe. When I stood triumphant to the front of the stage, I was met by thunderous applause for my "daring escapade." I never did confide, even to my family, the wherewithal behind this glamorous trick.

I reminisced over my one-and-only acting triumph the next evening as I ambled the country lanes after dinner. The sun had set early behind the mountain, and twilight fell fast around me. Summer cicadas and tree frogs started their nighttime chorus, and the wind brought a chill touch of fall to my skin when I found myself walking down a narrow green road not far from the inn. My pulse quickened when I realized that I had inadvertently ventured along the specter-haunted lane discussed so avidly in the barroom each night.

"Giants are a myth," I said aloud to reassure myself. "And ghostly giants even more so."

The words failed to reassure me. It is one thing to scoff at ghosts from the safety of a bar stool, and quite another to be walking downhill in the growing dark with the wind whistling around you, night creatures croaking and chirping and rustling mysteriously, and a mist slowly gathering in the lane ahead.

I paused and blinked, my mind finally catching up with my eyes. Mist was condensing several yards downhill from where I stood, filling most of the road and slowly towering up until it was a good ten feet high. The atmospheric conditions of this lovely summer evening not being conducive to mist or fog, I was hard pressed to understand what I was seeing, until the mist took the shape of a large humanoid creature whose head towered above me, even though I was a good fifteen feet above it on the upper slope of the road.

My heart started hammering in my chest. I was aware of the sudden silence. The night creatures were struck dumb. Only the wind whistled in my ear like the voice of the dead. My mouth went dry and my knees started knocking as I realized that granny had been correct about the existence of giants. I was face-to-chest with the specter of one. I threw my head back to stare into the face slowly forming in front of me. Two luminous dots were coalescing into glaring eyes above a craggy nose and a cruel, lipless mouth.

I had no idea what to do. Safety lay on the far side of the giant. Behind me was a narrow green lane and who knew what other dangers: bears, cougars, more ghosts? Still, retreat was probably my best option. Until I recalled the gray-eyed stranger saying the ghosts would vanish on their own. Maybe I could wait it out, I thought with a shudder, icy tendrils creeping down my spine.

A susurration from the nearby vegetation and flickers of white at the corners of my eyes drew my attention away from the massive specter before me. I turned my head and saw half a dozen small figures gathering in the road behind me. They made a chittering sound, like a half-seen mob preparing to tear something—or someone—apart. As in fact they were, for these were the victims of the giant, come to wreck their nightly revenge upon their murderous foe.

I did not think it possible, but the smaller gibbering ghosts were much more terrible than the giant ghost before me. They made retreat impossible, and the anger roiling off them was palpable in the night air. I gasped in fear as they swarmed me. The press of their cold hands sent frosty spikes right through my shirt and into my skin. The clammy feel of their fingers on my bare forearms was horrific.

Terror thrilled through my body, setting my feet moving forward without conscious volition. I had escaped a giant once before with a tremendous leap. I would do it again! Thought and action combined into a jump worthy of the most decorated athlete. I passed right through the ghostly giant's massive chest, which was colder than winter snow. The chill penetrated mind and body in the same coiling mists that my eyes beheld. I coughed and choked as my body cleared the monster and plummeted toward the road below. There was no stage crew this time with a blanket to save me. I crashed hard into the ground and my bouncing head slammed into a stone. I knew no more.

I learned afterward that my body was found upon the road by the gray-eyed farrier and carried back to the inn. The doctor who examined me found no broken bones, but I was so shaken up that the innkeeper's wife kept me abed the next day and dosed me with the doctor's foul-tasting decoctions. My lungs still felt full of ghostly mist and I could not take a deep breath.

After two full days in bed, I had finally recovered enough to sit down to supper in the dining room. I spent the meal trying—and failing—to logically explain away what had happened to me in the haunted lane. Ghosts and giants were myths. I'd seen a bit of fog forming and my imagination had created specters where none existed. It was an accident. I stumbled on a rock and knocked myself silly. My mind made many excuses, but my heart refused to believe any of them.

After supper, I went to the bar to enjoy a few drinks before bed. I needed something to calm my nerves. Every time I closed my eyes, I felt the clammy hands of the giant's victims touching me. And my lungs still felt heavy with the mist I'd swallowed when I jumped through the giant's chest. I shuddered and took refuge in another sip of my beer.

When the gray-eyed farrier came in with a friend from another district, I went over to thank him for his rescue. I was invited to join the men at their table, and we discussed everything from national events to the best produce to be found at the village market with equal interest.

And then the district man brought up the local ghost story, and I felt all the color drain from my face.

"Well, Jones," said he, "have you seen any more of your friend the ghost?"

The man's tone was jovial and disbelieving. Apparently, the supernatural was a frequent topic of debate between the farrier and his friend.

I felt the farrier's gray eyes flick toward me and then quickly away. "I wouldn't say the ghost is a friend, Nicholls," the farrier said easily. "But it happens that I did see it again last night."

My heart started racing and cold sweat beaded my forehead.

"You don't seem too bothered by your spectral encounter," said Nicholls, oblivious to the undercurrent at the table. My hands were shaking so badly that I set down my mug and tucked them in my lap.

"I've seen the ghost too many times to be ruffled when I encounter it," the farrier said laconically. "In my experience, it's folks who don't believe in spirits that have the most difficulty when they first meet one."

His gray eyes never strayed my way, but I knew this remark was aimed at me. The farrier continued, "Last night, however, the ghost was much changed from what it had been." He was still speaking to me, though Nicholls did not realize it. "When the giant rose before me on the road, his spirit form had a large hole right in the middle of its chest. I could see the moon shining through his ribcage, while the rest of him was misty as usual."

A Tremendous Leap

I choked and rushed out of the barroom as fast as my shaking legs would carry me. My chair crashed to the floor behind me and Nicholls cried: "Whatever is the matter with that chap?"

"Needs the privy, no doubt," Jones the farrier said, not a hint of merriment in his voice.

I fled outside and gulped clean air into my lungs, but this triggered my cough. I bent double, hacking away until I nearly threw up. At last, the spasms calmed. I dropped wearily to a garden bench, breathing deeply and shaking like a leaf.

As reason returned, I marveled at what the farrier had revealed. Great God in heaven! I'd permanently disfigured a ghost!

Just then, a heavy hand thumped my back, nearly startling me into another coughing fit. Jones joined me on the bench. "I have to hand it to you, lad. I've never heard of anyone changing a specter before," the gray-eyed farrier said with a small grin. "You may be the only person in this country who ever jumped through a ghost!"

Resources

"A Tremendous Leap." New Bern, NC: *New Berne Daily Times*, October 4, 1865.

Asfar, Daniel. *Ghost Stories of America*. Edmonton, Canada: Ghost House Books, 2001.

Barefoot, Daniel W. *Haints of the Hills*. Winston-Salem, NC: John F. Blair, Publishers, 2002.

———. *Piedmont Phantoms*. Winston-Salem, NC: John F. Blair, Publishers, 2002.

———. *Seaside Spectres*. Winston-Salem, NC: John F. Blair, Publishers, 2002.

Battle, Kemp P. *Great American Folklore*. New York: Doubleday, 1986.

Botkin, B. A., ed. *A Treasury of American Folklore*. New York: Crown, 1944.

Brewer, J. Mason. *American Negro Folklore*. Chicago: Quadrangle Books, 1972.

Brown, D. *Legends*. Eugene: Randall V. Mills Archive of Northwest Folklore at the University of Oregon, 1971.

Brunvand, Jan Harold. *The Choking Doberman and Other Urban Legends*. New York: W. W. Norton, 1984.

———. *The Vanishing Hitchhiker*. New York: W. W. Norton, 1981.

Coffin, Tristram P., and Hennig Cohen, eds. *Folklore in America*. New York: Doubleday & AMP, 1966.

———. *Folklore from the Working Folk of America*. New York: Doubleday, 1973.

Cohen, Daniel, and Susan Cohen. *Hauntings and Horrors*. New York: Dutton Children's Books, 2002.

Cooper, Horton. *North Carolina Mountain Folklore and Miscellany*. Murfreesboro, NC: Johnson Publishing, 1972.

Cornplanter, J. J. *Legends of the Longhouse.* Philadelphia: J. B. Lippincott, 1938.

Davis, Donald. *Southern Jack Tales.* Atlanta, GA: August House, Inc., 1992.

Dorson, R. M. *America in Legend.* New York: Pantheon Books, 1973.

Downer, Deborah L. *Classic American Ghost Stories.* Little Rock, AR: August House Publishers, 1990.

Duncan, Barbara R., ed. *Living Stories of the Cherokee.* Chapel Hill: The University of North Carolina Press, 1998.

———. *The Origin of the Milky Way & Other Living Stories of the Cherokee.* Chapel Hill: The University of North Carolina Press, 2008.

Editors of Life. *The Life Treasury of American Folklore.* New York: Time, 1961.

Erdoes, Richard, and Alfonso Ortiz. *American Indian Myths and Legends.* New York: Pantheon Books, 1984.

Flanagan, J. T., and A. P. Hudson. *The American Folk Reader.* New York: A. S. Barnes, 1958.

Foxfire Students. *Boogers, Witches, and Haints: Appalachian Ghost Stories. The Foxfire Americana Library.* New York: Anchor Books, 2011.

Hall, Joseph S. *Smoky Mountain Folks and Their Lore.* Asheville, NC: Gilbert Printing Co., 1960. Published in Cooperation with Great Smoky Mountains Natural History Association.

———. *Yarns and Tales from the Great Smokies.* Asheville, NC: The Cataloochee Press, 1978.

Hardin, John. *The Devil's Tramping Ground and Other North Carolina Mystery Stories.* Chapel Hill: University of North Carolina Press, 1949.

———. *Tar Heel Ghosts.* Chapel Hill: University of North Carolina Press, 1954.

Hauck, Dennis William. *Haunted Places: The National Directory.* New York: Penguin Books, 1996.

Resources

"Jock Brown's Ghost." Ironton, Missouri: *Iron County Register*, May 4, 1882.

Jones, Loyal, and Billy Edd Wheeler. *Curing the Cross-Eyed Mule.* Atlanta, GA: August House Publishers, 1989.

King, Duance H., ed. *The Memoirs of Lt. Henry Timberlake.* Cherokee, NC: Museum of the Cherokee Indian Press, 2007.

Leach, M. *The Rainbow Book of American Folk Tales and Legends.* New York: World Publishing, 1958.

Leeming, David, and Jake Pagey. *Myths, Legends, and Folktales of America.* New York: Oxford University Press, 1999.

Manly, Roger. *Weird Carolinas.* New York: Sterling Publishing, 2007.

Norman, Michael, and Beth Scott. *Historic Haunted America.* New York: Tor Books, 1995.

Peck, Catherine, ed. *A Treasury of North American Folk Tales.* New York: W. W. Norton, 1998.

Polley, J., ed. *American Folklore and Legend.* New York: Reader's Digest Association, 1978.

Reevy, Tony. *Ghost Train!* Lynchburg, VA: TLC Publishing, 1998.

Renegar, Michael. *Roadside Revenants and Other North Carolina Ghosts and Legends.* Fairview, NC: Bright Mountain Books, 2005.

Roberts, Nancy. *Ghosts of the Carolinas.* Columbia: University of South Carolina Press, 1962.

———. *North Carolina Ghosts and Legends.* Columbia: University of South Carolina Press, 1959.

Rule, Leslie. *Coast to Coast Ghosts.* Kansas City, KS: Andrews McMeel Publishing, 2001.

Russel, Randy, and Janet Barnett. *Mountain Ghost Stories and Curious Tales of Western North Carolina.* Winston-Salem, NC: John F. Blair, Publisher, 1988.

Schwartz, Alvin. *Scary Stories to Tell in the Dark.* New York: Harper Collins, 1981.

Skinner, Charles M. *American Myths and Legends.* Vol. 1. Philadelphia: J. B. Lippincott, 1903.

Resources

———. *Myths and Legends of Our Own Land*. Vols. 1–2. Philadelphia: J. B. Lippincott, 1896.

Spence, Lewis. *North American Indians: Myths and Legends Series*. London: Bracken Books, 1985.

Students of Haskell Institute. *Myths, Legends, Superstitions of North American Indian Tribes*. Cherokee, NC: Cherokee Publications, 1995.

Tanenbaum, Linda Duck, and Barry McGee. *Ghost Tales from the North Carolina Piedmont*. Winston-Salem, NC: Bandit Books, 2002.

Thay, Edrick. *Ghost Stories of North Carolina*. Auburn, WA: Lone Pine Publishing International, 2005.

———. *Ghost Stories of the Old South*. Auburn, WA: Lone Pine Publishing International, 2003.

Traylor, Ken, and Delas M. House Jr. *Asheville Ghosts and Legends*. Charleston, SC: Haunted America, 2006.

Walser, Richard. *North Carolina Legends*. Raleigh: Office of Archives and History, North Carolina Department of Cultural History, 1980.

Whedbee, Charles Harry. *Blackbeard's Cup and Stories of the Outer Banks*. Winston-Salem, NC: John F. Blair, Publisher, 1989.

———. *The Flaming Ship of Ocracoke and Other Tales of the Outer Banks*. Winston-Salem, NC: John F. Blair, Publisher, 1971.

———. *Legends of the Outer Banks and Tar Heel Tidewater*. Winston-Salem, NC: John F. Blair, Publisher, 1966.

———. *Outer Banks Mysteries and Seaside Stories*. Winston-Salem, NC: John F. Blair, Publisher, 1978.

———. *Outer Banks Tales to Remember*. Winston-Salem, NC: John F. Blair, Publisher, 1985.

White, D. *Folk Narratives*. Eugene: Randall V. Mills Archive of Northwest Folklore at the University of Oregon, 1971.

White, Newman Ivey, ed. *The Frank C. Brown Collection of North Carolina Folklore*. Durham, NC: Duke University Press, 1958.

Wigginton, Eliot, ed., and his students. *Foxfire 2*. New York: Anchor Books, 1973.

Resources

Wigginton, Eliot, ed. and Margie Bennett. *Foxfire 9*. New York: Anchor Books, 1986.

Wilson, Patty A. *Haunted North Carolina*. Mechanicsburg, PA: Stackpole Books, 2009.

Zeitlin, Steven J., Amy J. Kotkin, and Holly Cutting Baker. *A Celebration of American Family Folklore*. New York: Pantheon Books, 1982.

Zeple, Terrance. *Best Ghost Tales of North Carolina*. Sarasota, FL: Pineapple Press, 2006.

——— *Ghosts of the Carolina Coasts*. Sarasota, FL: Pineapple Press, 1999.

About the Author

S. E. Schlosser has been telling stories since she was a child, when games of "let's pretend" quickly built themselves into full-length tales acted out with friends. A graduate of Houghton College, the Institute of Children's Literature, and Rutgers University, she created

and maintains the award-winning website Americanfolklore .net, where she shares a wealth of stories from all fifty states, some dating back to the origins of America. She spends much of her time answering questions from visitors to the site. Many of her favorite emails come from other folklorists who delight in practicing the old tradition of "who can tell the tallest tale."

About the Illustrator

Artist Paul Hoffman trained in painting and printmaking, with his first extensive illustration work on assignment in Egypt, drawing ancient wall reliefs for the University of Chicago. His work graces books of many genres—children's titles, textbooks, short story collections, natural history volumes, and numerous cookbooks. For *Spooky North Carolina*, he employed a scratchboard technique and an active imagination.

253